THE
DRUG LORDS

America's Pharmaceutical Cartel

by Tonda R. Bian

ISBN 0-9654568-0-3
Library of Congress CCN 96-092687

Published by No Barriers Publishing
1201 S Westnedge Ave
Kalamazoo, Michigan 49008
Printed in the United States of America

Produced with assistance from
Griffith Publishing, Caldwell, Idaho

Dedication

To Michael, who helped me
see the realities of health care
in this country and who
believed in this project, as I
have, from the beginning, and
to mom and dad, who just
believed.

Acknowledgements

As the work on the development of this book comes to an end, I'd like to thank friends, family and others for their help and support with this project.

To Joyce Griffith of Griffith Publishing for her patient work; to Catherine Erickson for her excellent timing in helping me fill a crucial gap in information; to Sophia Asmar and Jennie Epitropoulos for their help and input on the cover and to Sue Regonini and Miriam Griffith for the cover design; to Sam Epitropoulos for his pride in this work; to Joan Copeland for her friendship and for always being exactly where she is needed; to Rick Bauer for his friendship; to Dr. Dick Versendaal for his pioneering spirit and inspiration; to Dr. Michael Epitropoulos for his constant encouragement, input and needed pushes to finish the book; to Nick and Fern Bian, my parents, for just about everything; and to Alexa, my daughter, who was not in my life when this project started, did her best to keep me from finishing it, but who always reminded me what is most important.

Finally, much of the credit for this project belongs to the thousands of professionals who practice preventive healthcare in spite of the stifling politics they are forced to confront daily.

Contents

Prologue

The television commercial shows a pharmaceutical researcher working late into the night. In a close-up shot we see her agonizing as she searches for the answer, the solution—perhaps the cure—for a deadly, dreaded disease. She is a no-bones, serious woman, dedicated to her work, dedicated to her search to help end human suffering. She looks fatigued because she has probably been working without a break for hours, a day, maybe more. Yet before our eyes, she says what we had only hoped to hear. As she peers through her microscope and then backs off with a look of bone-weary relief, she pulls at the viewers' heartstrings with these words: "There it is. There it is!" The answer she and her pharmaceutical employer have labored so long to find—yet another important answer to human illness.

The pharmaceutical industry would like us to absorb this picture of altruism, this image of their never-ending quest for better health for each of us. The truth, however, is that the industry has long taken advantage of the public's belief that medicine and all its affiliated concerns are totally sincere.

That belief, unfortunately, is a myth because the pharmaceutical industry is as profit-motivated as any other company on Wall Street. Its primary interest is wealth, not health. With their thousands of drugs, the pharmaceutical industry has never proved that good health comes in a pill, a shot, or a bottle of medicine. What they have proved is that they can convince a naïve public that it does.

Overview

How safe would you feel taking your next medication if you knew that hundreds of thousands of people die each year due to reactions from drugs their doctors prescribe and that millions of others experience serious side effects due to drug complications?

How would you feel if you knew that the drugs prescribed for you hold the dangerous possibility of interacting with other prescriptions or even common over-the-counter drugs and that your doctor might be completely unaware of this health- or life-threatening potential?

How comfortable would you feel if you knew your doctor gained most of the information he or she has obtained about drugs through pharmaceutical company representatives, pharmaceutical-sponsored seminars and advertising paid for exclusively by pharmaceutical companies?

What you *should* feel is "unsafe," because this is the ominous side of the "legal" drug industry. No matter how exhaustive the research, development and testing criteria in the drug approval process may appear to be, there are gaping holes in drug regulation and far too much sidestepping by the pharmaceutical industry.

Ironically, all of this continues with the full cooperation of the powerful government arm known as the FDA (Food and Drug Administration).

Enter the dark side of health care, the side ruled by the highest priority of making money rather than making people healthy; by the side that renders MD's and DO's powerless without a prescription pad; the side populated with drug companies that continuously beat lawsuits brought on by families of injured and deceased people; the side that prefers to deal with sick people and not those who are well because there is more money to be made in treating the sick and dying.

The Drug Lords shoots a critical look at our over-pre-scribed, over-medicated society and the role the pharma-ceutical industry plays in keeping us there. The book also accuses medicine of breaking antitrust laws, of preventing other avenues of health care from competing with estab-lished medicine—all with the full approval and assistance of the United States government.

1

Gambling With a Medical Monopoly

Theodore Mianaris is dead. His battle with chronic liver disease was long and courageous, but in the end he is dead. Doctors gave him his death sentence in 1991, telling him he had six months to live. They put him on the drug Lasix and sent him home to die. Still, three years later, he was alive, primarily because of lifestyle changes that slowly seemed to be strengthening him—but then just when he was beginning to feel optimistic, the Mayo Clinic told him there were tumors on his liver.

He sought a second opinion at a Pittsburgh medical center where he was told his tumors were cancerous and he would need chemotherapy. He took one treatment, was given medication and went home.

Up until the Mayo Clinic, the patient was feeling stronger, his energy had improved and although there were frequent setbacks, he sensed a gain in his health. Then came the new diagnosis, confirmation in Pittsburgh and the chemotherapy. This therapy itself played havoc with his body, weakening him and creating severe bloating, jaundice and extreme fatigue.

A month later when he returned to Pittsburgh, he learned his doctor was out of town and that another would step in. During that visit, Ted was scheduled for another diagnostic test, but hospital communications were poor and he was given breakfast. Because he had breakfast, the test could not be administered. He would have to stay another day, but at his own expense, not the hospital's.

The substitute doctor decided that chemotherapy might not be the best idea since the patient's bilirubin levels (liver enzymes) appeared too high. Ironically, the levels during the second visit were approximately the same as they were during the first visit when the original doctor thought chemotherapy was the best method of treatment.

Instead of chemotherapy, the substitute doctor sent Ted home with yet another medication, one used to dissolve gall stones. The drug, Actigall, had been contraindicated (not to be used) for patients with chronic liver disease in the 1990 edition of the *Physicians' Desk Reference*. Yet in more current editions of the *Physicians' Desk Reference*, that contraindication is absent. By the end of the first week of taking the drug, Ted's liver function had worsened, he became incoherent and pre-comatose. PDR guidelines or not, the drug was toxic for this patient.

The patient's wife called Pittsburgh with the emergency, but neither of his doctors could be reached. It was a mere communications staff member at the medical center who agreed that it was a good idea for Ted to stop taking the drug. The patient's condition spiraled downward following the Actigall incident, an incident never addressed by the medical center, an incident that did not even prompt a call from the hospital to the patient. His bill for the visit that his family believed killed him came to thousands of dollars.

Less than three months after the Mayo Clinic diagnosis and weeks after the Pittsburgh Actigall fiasco, Theodore Mianaris died.

In the summer of 1995, the medical center contacted the Mianaris family to see how the patient was doing. He had been dead one year at that time.

All parties involved would argue opposing cases. The hospital would say its physician did not compromise the patient's health because the PDR did not note a contraindication with liver disease in its current edition. Their likely position was that, "He was dying anyway. The illness probably killed him." The patient's family would say the doctors should have known better. Yet, perhaps both parties are right and a third is at fault—that party being the one alleging research that showed "no complication with Actigall and liver disease patients." Who could benefit from such a conclusion? A pharmaceutical interest, perhaps?

For years, stories and statistics of medical abuse have proven startling. Today medical abuse, negligence, and injury or death due to inappropriate medical intervention are epidemic.

As far back as 1964, Dr. Elihu Schimmell, MD, who conducted what is known as the Yale New Haven Hospital Study, reported shocking findings:

> **At least 100,000 people die annually from reactions or complications from medications; the actual number could run as high as 200,000 deaths per year. This, combined with deaths resulting from other medical procedures raises the estimated total to between 156,000 to 260,000 deaths each year.**

In 1965, Leighton Cluff, MD, in his work in a John Hopkins study, found that 14 percent of all hospital patients had their stay prolonged due to medical reactions.

Although conducted in the 1960s, these studies bring to light an emerging picture of the healthcare situation that has geometrically escalated in the final years of the twenty-first century. The reason? When we consider the thousands of drugs that have been put on the market and the significant increase in medical intervention over the past thirty years, we can begin to comprehend the staggering opportunity for abuse. A frightening picture of medicine's effect on the health and welfare of a nation comes into focus.

Older findings of medical abuse pale in comparison to more recent research including a five-year study conducted by Howard Hiatt, Dean of Public Health, Harvard University, and commissioned by the state of New York. Completed at a cost of $3.1 million, the 1990 study became one of the most comprehensive reviews of malpractice ever undertaken in the United States. Its findings:

> Medical negligence in 1984 alone caused 7,000 hospital deaths and an additional 99,000 injuries, translating into an economic loss of $894 million. The authors point out that these numbers include only those in the State of New York and represent deaths where causes range from medication to surgical complication. Projections nationwide would shed an even clearer light on medical negligence.[1]

Comparing figures from the Yale New Haven and John Hopkins studies in 1964-65 to those found in the Harvard study in 1990, a dismal picture of healthcare quality in the 1990s becomes clear.

Experts critical of the established medical community are saying that the healthcare crisis today is not only a matter of access barriers due to cost, but more significantly, a crisis in the quality of care provided.

This view of orthodox medicine does not come from critics outside the medical profession alone, but from a significant number of respected members within its ranks. Among these critics is Dr. Joseph D. Beasley, an MD who in his 700-page Kellogg report points to the failures of traditional or orthodox health care as it exists in the United States today.

> There cannot be much doubt that modern medicine's paradigm and the resulting methodology are failing us on the most critical front, the spread of chronic disabling and killer diseases. With its classical science paradigm and methods of specific etiology—it is shooting arrows at the storm. It neglects newer systemic findings about nutrition, behavior, and human ecology... In the struggle with degenerative disease it is hamstrung by its

hyperspecialization and tunnel vision. In sum,
modern medicine is growing progressively
narrow, ineffectual, and expensive.[2]

Critics believe responsibility lies along a cross section
of medicine: those medical professionals who diagnose, treat,
perform surgery and those who manufacture prescription
and over-the-counter drugs. Many critics pin the responsibility on a profession that in large part exists in a medi-pod
of self-satisfaction, refusing to look outside its own scope of
study to arenas that might shed light on disease, primarily
for fear of loss of income and possible loss of a god-like power.
The failure of modern medicine can be seen as an antitrust
issue, with the medical profession working to hold a monopoly by labeling their work and their work alone as scientific, and only what they do as acceptable healthcare.

Ralph Moss, Ph.D., author of the book *The Cancer
Chronicles*, spoke at the Adjuvant Nutrition in Cancer
Treatment Symposium in Tulsa Oklahoma, in November
of 1992. "We have a bankrupt medical system," he said.
"...bankrupt economically and intellectually." He accuses
the traditional medical community of close mindedness, of
bias toward alternatives that challenge traditional medicine, and of suppression of information medical practitioners know is valid concerning alternative methods.

In a professional profile in the newsletter *Prescription
for Health,* Moss makes clear his disenchantment with medicine that began during his tenure with the Sloan-Kettering
Cancer Center in New York. Working as an assistant director of public affairs during the mid-1970s, he witnessed
research on laetrile, a by-product of apricot pits and a potential cancer-fighting substance.

Sloan-Kettering research, Moss said, offered promis-
ing results, where tests showed laetrile inhibiting metastasis (spread of cancer through the body) to the lungs of animals afflicted with breast cancer. With laetrile, metastasis
to the lungs was present in just 20 percent of animals researched, compared to 80 to 90 percent of subjects without
laetrile.

Yet, even with this breakthrough finding, Sloan-
Kettering halted the research. According to Moss, Sloan-

Kettering officials falsified results of the research project, reporting that their findings with laetrile found nothing of any significance. Moss stated that he himself was instructed to lie about the research.

Moss refused to comply with Sloan-Kettering directives and instead held a press conference the next day to report what he had personally observed and what had happened at the cancer center. He was subsequently fired for allegedly failing to fulfill his work responsibilities.

Moss went on to publish a book, *The Cancer Industry*, a work based on the "big" business of cancer. He states that no one has ever successfully refuted the message his text carried.

In Moss's opinion, much of what the medical community calls "quackery" interprets into modes of treatment that might well be viable, but the medical community will not give it its seal of approval because it is either not their own or they have no stake in its success. They cannot corner the market, so they ignore the treatment and continue to benefit from the millions of dollars sent to them for research, dollars funded through donations and taxes.

Moss relates another experience that occurred at Sloan-Kettering in which one of the center's vice presidents told him of a major source for new medical ideas. The officer proceeded to show Moss a book entitled, *Unproven Methods of Cancer Management*, which Moss says was officially labeled by the medical establishment as the "quack list" of the American Cancer Society. In spite of this, the vice president told him that the book was a source of a significant number of ideas for cancer research, a kind of medical bible of nontraditional treatments the cancer community publicly decries.

Medicine traditionally disavows methods of treatment it has not created or promoted and historically creates professional pariahs out of its own members who choose to pursue alternative methods including Andrew Ivy, a dean of the University of Illinois Medical Center in Chicago. As a highly respected cancer doctor, Ivy was discredited in the 1950s when he advocated an immune therapy for cancer.[3]

In light of medicine's stranglehold on healthcare, there is a sense of frustration and anger shared by healthcare professionals who believe the United States is losing the healthcare war not only financially, but ethically, morally and, most importantly, in the quality of care itself. Dr. Samuel Epstein, an occupational-environmental medicine professor who has served on the faculty at the University of Illinois, co-authored with Moss a "Comment" piece that was published on the opinion page of *USA Today* in December of 1991.

Here is a portion of that letter.

On December 23, 1971, President Nixon signed the National Cancer Act. The 'War Against Cancer' was inaugurated, and the cure for cancer was promised by the Bicentennial. Twenty years, billions of dollars and millions of deaths later, no cure is in sight. We're losing the war.

Epstein and Moss went on to note that cancer now strikes one in three Americans, killing one in four. This translates into 500,000 deaths in 1990 alone. "Our ability to cure most advanced cancers scarcely has improved since 1971. For example, the five-year survival rate for non-localized breast cancer remains a static 18 percent." The men also pointed to the "cancer establishment" whom they charged with pushing highly toxic and expensive drugs marketed by pharmaceutical interests who have close relationships with cancer centers. The men ask, "Is it any wonder [cancer centers and drug companies] refuse to investigate innovative approaches developed outside their own institutions?"

The *USA Today* piece also includes the finding that in 1990, the Office of Technology Assessment knew of 200 scientific studies which supported this nepotistic effort between cancer centers and pharmaceutical interests, but at the time of the commentary, the National Cancer Institute (NCI) had not taken action.

Moss and Epstein believe the war against cancer needs a complete overhaul where prevention is the highest priority. They also believe that until prevention is the priority,

Congress should refuse to fund the NCI and the public should boycott the "Bloated American Cancer Society." The pair call it a needed grass-roots movement.[4]

For all of the resistance to natural and nontoxic alternatives, Moss places the lion's share of the blame on pharmaceutical companies, observing that "drug companies want the highest cost medical system." He also notes that these companies represent some of the most powerful lobbies in Washington today and work with all aspects of the medical community to keep their products available and highly visible to the public.[5]

The irony of high cost medicine is the simple fact that its very effectiveness is questionable. Social critic Ivan Illich in his book *Medical Nemesis: The Expropriation of Health*, writes this:

> In 1962, when the United States Food and Drug Administration began to examine the 4,300 prescription drugs that had appeared since World War II, only 2 out of 5 were found effective ... Fewer than 98% of these chemical substances constitute valuable contributions to the pharmacopeia used in primary care.[6]

One Harvard-bred medical doctor, Andrew Weil, serves as another outspoken critic on orthodox care in this country. While an instructor of alternative medicine, mind-body interactions and medical botany at the University of Arizona College of Medicine, Weil noted that modern medicine's worst practice is the overuse of medications. Synthetic medicines, he warns, are often dangerous with side effects that range from harmless to fatal.

Weil mentions that it is this knowledge that frightens the public and the reason that of all prescriptions written today, at least half are never filled. He believes people are turning from prescription medicine to alternative care, not at the urging of their medical doctors, but as a result of their own search for more effective, safer treatment.

Weil uses a variety of alternative methods and some orthodox ones in treating his patients, prescribing 40 to

50 herbal medicines for every pharmaceutical prescription he writes. Weil's experience has shown him that herbal applications are safe and dilute, taking visibly longer than drugs to work on symptoms, but much less toxic.

Weil refers to the basking of the orthodox medical community in a god-like complacency and resolve while they turn a critical eye to ideas they do not know, ideas that have not been proven effective in allegedly scientific studies.

His experience tells him that what is taught in most medical schools today is not relevant and what is relevant is not taught. "Each department [within medical schools] has such a vested interest in its own agenda that there is no room for new information and alternative approaches."

Weil believes that medicine will not change without public pressure on both medicine and insurance companies. Since insurance companies decide what they will and will not pay for, the insured person is at their mercy. While the patient might want, for example, to seek alternative care in acupuncture or hypnotherapy for high blood pressure, few insurance firms pay for these; instead the person may be encouraged to fill a prescription for blood pressure medication, not because it is necessarily the best route for treatment, but because it is something insurance will cover.[7]

One well-known medical doctor has come under constant fire for his work in what he calls complementary medicine—a blend of alternative and orthodox methods. Dr. Robert Atkins, the man whose diet advice propelled him to prominence, has been bombarded by established medicine through the years, medicine saying his methods are dangerous and have even resulted in deaths.

Using methods including ozone therapy, vitamins and diet, Atkins believes his method of treating patients is less harmful than surgery, chemotherapy and radiation. In an article written by Gale Scott of *Newsday*, Atkins remarks that "Cancer itself isn't so horrible; it's the treatment. People know what their options are if they choose orthodox medicine. That's why they come to me."

Dr. Atkins fills his prescriptions through his own retail operation and mail-order business, which his critics see as unethical. "Having somebody [such as Dr. Atkins] pushing something they have a financial stake in is dangerous," says Bruce Jennings, executive director of the Hastings Institute.[8]

Dangerous? Unethical? On the other side, nontraditional care givers have cause to ask what the difference is between Dr. Atkins's mail order medical service and the practice of medical doctors accepting free trips, dinners, gifts and even alleged monetary kickbacks such as purchasing incentives offered by pharmaceutical companies.

Turn on almost any talk show or pick up just about any news magazine, and you can observe the battle raging between traditional and nontraditional healthcare. A December 15, 1992 airing of a Phil Donahue show pitted traditional MDs against those who have chosen the nonmedical route. The basic argument against nontraditional practitioners from the orthodox side was, "Prove that your methods work. Prove that your nonmedical treatments are not a waste of money, a way to fool the public."

George Guess, an MD appearing on the show and a practitioner of homeopathic medicine, was ready with a retort. "[Medical authorities ask us] *Where is it published?*" he said. "Again I want to emphasize, in 1978, the Office of Technology Assessment did a review of prevailing medical procedures and found 80 percent of them had no scientific justification."

Dr. Guess made the statement to point out that most medical procedures have not been proven, and that there are no specific answers to why or how they are said to work, but those medical procedures are still used. Yet, when it comes to nonmedical procedures, the medical community attacks practices such as homeopathy saying, "There is no proof these methods work." Apparently a standard of proof applies only to the "other" side, not to advocates of traditional medicine.

The homeopathic doctors on the panel asserted that the FDA does not allow manufacturers of nonmedical treatments to make claims about their products, nor does the FDA allow the practitioners who prescribe them to assert that a particular vitamin, herb or remedy will, for example, help to strengthen the heart. The homeopaths said they felt that this restriction is a technique the medical community uses to curtail and inhibit the public's understanding of non-pharmaceutical products.

Yet, efforts to inhibit public trust in nonmedical avenues appear to be ineffective. The *New England Journal of Medicine* issued a report early in 1992 stating that Americans now visit alternative practitioners more often than they do medical doctors. One of every three people in the U.S. now seeks alternative care.

The medical community's reaction to this news was to proclaim that doctors have a legal responsibility to determine the safety and efficacy of alternative therapies. This was the specific response by M. Roy Schwarz, the American Medical Association's vice president for science.[9]

With these examples, the premise for *The Drug Lords* takes shape: There can be no healthcare reform in this country without a new perspective and a different type of investigation aimed at medical ethics, at the potential conspiracy between doctors, pharmaceutical companies, institutions of medical research, hospitals, and insurance companies. That investigation must focus on whether the interest of the patient is at the center of concern and at the center of decision making. If the focus is found to be on the gloved hand, if it is determined that medicine is most interested in profiting at the expense of the patient, then the real problem in American healthcare will emerge.

Physicians pledge the Hippocratic oath named for the ancient Greek philosopher Hippocrates—to take care of the sick in the best way they know possible and to do no harm. If a growing number of critics are right and a conspiracy exists, the nature of medicine stands in line not with Hippocrates but with the ancient Greek word "hypokrites," the word now known as "hypocrite"—one who affects virtues or qualities he does not have, a dissembler, an actor, a sham.[10]

1. Yale New Haven Study (1964), John Hopkins Study (1965), and Harvard University study (1990) taken from information provided by Chester Wilk, D.C., 5130 Belmont Avenue, Chicago, IL 60641.

2. "Nutrition-Oriented Physician to speak at AANP Convention," an article by Terry Lemerond focusing on Joseph D. Beasley, MD, *Prescription For Health* (newsletter), August 1992, Vol. 4, No.8.

3. Interview with Ralph Moss, Ph.D., "Health Writer Pushing for Change," *Prescription for Health* (newsletter), February 1993, Vol. 5. No. 2.

4. "Losing the Cancer War," an Opinion USA submission, *USA Today*, December 23, 1991.

5. Interview with Ralph Moss, *Prescription for Health* (newsletter), February 1993.

6. *Medical Nemesis, the Expropriation of Health*, Ivan Illich, Pantheon Books, New York, 1976, p. 74.

7. "Natural Selection," an article focusing on Andrew Weil, MD, written by Bill Krasean, and published in the *Kalamazoo Gazette*, October 27, 1992.

8. Article focusing on Dr. Robert Atkins, written by Gale Scott, *Newsday,* (date unknown).

9. Study conducted by Dr. David Eisenberg, Beth Israel Hospital, 1990, and a related editorial reported in the *New England Journal of Medicine*, January 28, 1993.

10. *Webster's New Collegiate Dictionary*.

2

Medicine For Sale— An Image at Risk

In 1992 the American Medical Association launched a major public relations campaign with the goal of boosting the sagging image of the medical community in the United States. The campaign was the AMA's crisis management reaction to a public who increasingly believes the quality of healthcare in the United States isn't what it should be. The effort was also the AMA's reaction to the public's growing movement toward nonmedical treatment.

The campaign included print ads featuring individual doctors with headlines reading, "I have never gotten used to people dying. And I don't want to get used to it." The copy of one of these ads continued as follows:

> Dr. Aliza Lifshitz, Internist, Los Angeles,
> California, Member, American Medical
> Association.

Patients come to physicians for many reasons. Beyond relief from pain, they seek compassion, empathy and support. AIDS patients receive all of these and more from Dr. Aliza Lifshitz. Born and raised in Mexico and educated at one of Mexico City's finest medical schools, Dr. Lifshitz now serves the Hispanic community in Southern California. Over one third of her patients have tested HIV positive. Most live below the poverty level. Many are illegal aliens. 'I never forgot what it means to be a doctor, and what it means is embodied in the Principles of Medical Ethics of the American Medical Association (AMA),' states Dr. Lifshitz. Dr. Lifshitz is a testament to what is best in medicine. She is also a member of the AMA.

This ad was focused on recruiting new members. Other efforts of the campaign were aimed at doctors willing to go to the public to speak and act as spokespeople for the AMA. Other public relations efforts the AMA initiated included a joint venture with *Good Housekeeping* to produce a consumer health magazine and the establishing of a partnership with CNBC cable network to increase weekly medical programming.

Many state associations also initiated their own campaigns to boost image and counteract falling public confidence in medicine. These public relations campaigns came on the heels of an AMA poll that found that 69 percent of the public had lost faith in their doctors, up from 64 percent just three years earlier in 1989.

According to Terry A. Rondberg, D.C. (Doctor of Chiropractic), and president of the World Chiropractic Alliance, "It's clear that medical doctors recognize that their popularity is shrinking. They realize people no longer automatically turn to drugs and surgery for the answer. The AMA is looking for ways to counter the mass exodus to non-allopathic forms of health care. Obviously, it's going to try to control the media to do that."[1]

Authors of a *New England Journal of Medicine* article expressed the same concern when it published findings from the Eisenburg/Beth Israel Hospital study. Edward Campion, MD, commented in an editorial in the same edition that, "The reason people go to nonmedical practitioners is simple: they want to feel better. Access is easy. Invitations to be healed are everywhere. It's cheaper than seeing a physician." The editorial also stated, " In addition, many are dissatisfied with the medical establishment. Though Americans want all that modern medicine can deliver, they also fear it. They may resent the way visits to physicians quickly lead to pills, tests, and technology. Most now know of iatrogenic disasters from medicine gone wrong. Consumers also may seek out unconventional healers because they think their problems will be taken more seriously. They receive the benefit of attention, with invitations to return often." In the same piece, the author writes, "The public's expensive romance with unconventional medicine is cause for our profession to worry. We need to demonstrate more effectively our dedication to caring for the whole patient—worries, quirks, and all."[2]

The *New England Journal of Medicine* article reported that more than one-third (34 percent) of Americans used at least one form of unconventional therapy in the last year, and that one-third of these people saw providers for the therapy. Patients who consulted alternative care providers averaged 19 visits at an average cost of $28 per visit, for a total of 425 million visits, compared with 388 million visits made to all family doctors, internists and other primary-care physicians.

Of significance is that the expenditures associated with these 425 million visits to practitioners of unconventional care amount to $13.7 billion, of which $10.3 billion or three quarters of the total was paid directly by the patients, not by insurance funds or other third-party payers. The *Journal* notes that this figure is comparable to the $12.8 billion the public paid in out-of-pocket dollars for all hospitalizations in the U.S. that year.[3]

Proponents of nonconventional care say these figures attest to the growing faith in nonmedical treatment, or at the least the willingness of the public to find methods that are more useful to them.

Holding on to patients, keeping their confidence, and maintaining damage control are keys to success in the medical community. Doctors are not to be blamed for engaging

in a public relations effort, a necessary element for any organization hoping to survive and thrive. The AMA and the
medical community it represents do what they feel is necessary to meet the competition. Yet a substantial number
of analysts feel that medicine in general is guilty of ethical
lapses, including—

1. **Misleading the public into believing it alone holds
the answers to better health**

2. **Taking undue credit for every gain in health by
implying that improvements are due to the efforts of
physicians**

3. **Attempting to convey that medical practitioners
have only sincere and honorable intentions.**

Medicine's public relations campaigns, including those
of pharmaceutical interests, could be paraphrased, "If only
we can find the answers to the dreaded diseases we so des-
perately are trying to find, your health will be assured."
(As in the image-building commercial referenced at the
beginning of this book, showing a pharmaceutical researcher
working late into the night, looking tired and stressed when
finally, she says, "*There* it is!")

Critical observers charge that this image of "sincerity"
is in large part a ploy that has served the medical industry
well, paving the way for huge profits that it enjoys without
improving the quality of care.

Another example is seen in an ad placed by the Pharmaceutical Manufacturers Association. The copy for the ad
reads, "With each passing decade, people have been able to
hold onto more of life's rich moments. In 1950, the average
life span of men was 65. Today, it's approaching 80, due in
many ways to advances in medicine. At the forefront are
pharmaceutical companies who are making America's largest investment in drug research."

Two claims are stated in this commercial: first, that
there has been an increase of fifteen years in man's life
expectancy since 1950 and, second, that this miracle is due
primarily to the dedication of the pharmaceutical industry.

Both claims can be questioned. According to *Statistical
Bulletin*, the bi-monthly MetLife publication, the life ex-

pectancy at birth for all males and females born in the U.S. in 1990 is 75.4 years.

The discrepancy of 4.6 years between 75.4 years and 80 years could perhaps be overlooked since the advertisement uses the phrase, "approaching 80." But there is no mention of the fact that life expectancy in the United States ranks eleventh among selected industrialized countries, following Japan at 78.9 years (1990 study); Iceland at 78.0 years (1989-90 study); Sweden at 77.6 years (1990 study); Switzerland at 77.4 years (1989-90 study), and others.[4]

Here we see the pharmaceutical industry cheerfully taking credit for dramatically extending life expectancy, even though those gains are not that significant when viewed in context with other countries. More importantly, they omit giving any credit to factors such as improved diet and increased exercise that might play a more significant role in extended life expectancy than pharmaceutical breakthroughs. Even if pharmaceutical products can be shown to be partially responsible for a prolonged lifespan, is there any evidence indicating that these products have improved the quality of life rather than just the quantity of years lived?

The second point of the ad in question is the claim that "pharmaceutical companies. . .are making America's largest investment in drug research." Perhaps this is an accurate statement, but since research directed by private pharmaceutical interests is supplemented by government research and since the industry's research dollars reap huge profits to the drug companies, the investment could be seen as less than altruistic.

Taxpayer-funded research provided $2 million toward the development of the AIDS drug AZT through the National Institute of Health's National Cancer Institute. Subsequently, Burroughs Wellcome gained the exclusive patent on AZT and has made an estimated $1.4 billion in profits from the drug, according to the publication *Public Citizen*, of the Ralph Nader-founded organization of the same name. (Public Citizen, Jan/Feb 1993)[5]

On a more recent note, the television magazine "Day One," reported in their October 18, 1993 program that AZT has been found to be of little therapeutic value in treating AIDS patients.[6]

Another issue involving drug research involves Ceradase, once called a breakthrough treatment for the sometimes fatal genetic disorder known as Gaucher's disease. According to a *Time* magazine article,

> Ceradase and the Massachusetts company called Genzyme that makes it, illustrate how drug companies have turned government research and regulations into big business.
>
> The Federal Government financed the discovery of the drug and then paid tax dollars so that entrepreneurs could learn how to manufacture it. Now [the Federal Government] is paying as much as 20 percent of the nation's Ceradase bill through Medicare and Medicaid. And Ceradase isn't the only high-priced drug that has flowed from government laboratories. The new chemotherapeutic Taxol, as well as almost half of all other cancer drugs, owes its existence to government scientists, as do nearly all AIDS drugs."

The *Time* article notes that the government paid an estimated 20 percent of total research costs on Ceradase. (Genzyme, the biotechnology firm that manufactures Ceradase, insists the pricetag is closer to 14 percent.)

Genzyme now claims that the process of extracting an enzyme from human placental tissue makes the drug so expensive that it is pushing the cost of the drug to $350,000 per year, per patient.

Some analysts say that the price tag set by Genzyme is a clear result of simple corporate greed and misuse of government research dollars. Henry Termeer, chairman of the Board at Genzyme, defends his company's pricing by telling *Time* that the price wasn't set based on greed, but on the fact that development and manufacturing investments give the company little flexibility regarding cost.

Dick Thompson's *Time* article also pointed out criticism Genzyme has received for its marketing tactics for Ceradase, which have included contacting Gaucher's victims and their doctors directly with videos and literature claiming their product can bring sufferers a healthy, pain-free life. But those who have bought the product include only an estimated 800 out of 11,000 patients who need treatment for the disease. Most who don't use the drug find the cost prohibitive.[7]

Looking at government spending for the Ceradase development price tag—$9 million of the total—and superimposing this figure on the small number of Gaucher victims able to obtain the drug (800 people), the question must be asked, "Where is the sense in developing a drug that is only accessible to a small number of people?"

In a related *Time* article, John Greenwald noted that Henry Waxman, Democratic congressman from California, attacked the pharmaceutical industry by unveiling an Office of Technology Assessment report. That report stated the drug industry has raked in $2 billion dollars in excess profits each year and "lavished vast sums on 'wasteful' campaigns to encourage doctors to prescribe pricey medications." Looking at this, critics charge that pharmaceutical companies cannot be hurting much by the "excessive" dollars they spend on research.

Greenwald noted that these attacks "stunned the $75 billion U.S. pharmaceutical industry, long the country's most profitable manufacturing sector and one of its last world leaders in developing new products."[8]

As a result of this growing scrutiny, leaders in the pharmaceutical industry watched their collective stock value fall 15 percent by early 1993. They responded with an aggressive campaign defending their products and practices.

A point of ethics should be raised regarding pharmaceutical interest ads. The question is whether medicine is practicing good business and good marketing, or whether it is involved in gross mismanagement of public responsibility. Many believe the latter to be true, that medicine holds a much greater ethical and public responsibility than do manufacturers of blue jeans or mouthwash. Truth in advertising and fair business practice must be linked in tandem when an issue as vital as public health is concerned.

An example of questionable advertising by the industry involves a full-page ad with the headline, "To the American People From the People Who Work In Pharmaceutical Companies."

The ad focuses on a number of statements supporting the drug industry and their commitment to quality affordable healthcare in the wake of President Clinton's promise to reform the healthcare delivery system in the United States. Statements prepared by this pharmaceutical interest group include the claim that:

> **Increases in the price of prescription drugs are not a major cause of America's spiraling healthcare expenditures.**

The ad went on to say that pharmaceuticals represent less than 7 percent of the total healthcare bill in this country each year, and that while healthcare costs have escalated to 14 percent of the Gross National Product, pharmaceuticals have consistently accounted for less than 1 percent of the GNP for decades.

Rebuttal: According to the Consumer Price Index, pharmaceutical products rose an average of 10 percent per year between 1981 and 1991 surpassed in average increase only by the rise in hospital room costs. Drugs also represent the largest out-of-pocket healthcare expense for Americans.

Another claim in the ad read:

> **Contrary to recent reports from a Senate committee, pharmaceutical companies who voluntarily pledged to limit price increases have been true to their word.**

Rebuttal: The question here is just how many drug companies made a pledge to hold price increases to the levels of the Consumer Price Index. It is reported that only 10 of the more than 100 pharmaceutical companies have publicly made this pledge. These companies represent approximately 40 percent of the prescription drug market. In other words, a voluntarily commitment, though, not set in stone, was made that manufacturers with 40 percent of all pharmaceutical sales would restrain price increases. What about the 90 plus manufacturers with the other 60 percent of the legal drug market who haven't even attempted to work with the request?

An addendum to this subject: By early 1993, a Senate committee had already charged Merck & Company with raising drug prices faster than inflation. Merck hotly disputed the charge.[9]

Another claim:

> Although Americans pay more for some drugs than the citizens of other countries, Americans actually work significantly fewer hours to pay their average annual bill for pharmaceuticals than do citizens of many other industrial nations.

Rebuttal: The General Accounting Office released a report showing that Canadian subsidiaries of American pharmaceutical companies were charging 32 percent less for the same drugs in Canada than they were in the United States. Here is a sampling appearing in an October 1992 *New York Times* article by Milt Freudenheim:

Drug price comparisons: US and Canada (1992)

Drug and manufacturer	Therapeutic use	U.S. price compared with price in Canada
Xanax (Upjohn)	anti-anxiety	183% higher
Zantac (Glaxo)	anti-ulcer	30% higher
Premarin [Wyeth Ayerst]	estrogen therapy	162% higher

After the General Accounting Office released these figures, another cost comparison was made by Stephen Schondelmeyer, who studies pharmaceutical economics at the University of Minnesota. He found that by July of 1992, Xanax was 225 percent higher, Zantac was 40 percent higher and Premarin 190 percent higher in the United States than in Canada.

In all, the General Accounting Office study of 121 drugs found that only 23 of the drugs were lower in the U.S., while 98 were higher, generally by 50 percent or more.

American drug manufacturers contested the finding saying that the comparisons weren't accurate because factors such as wholesale prices and varying sizes and tablet dosages were not paid attention to.

Rep. Henry Waxman of California, who served on a U.S. House sub-committee that examined drug prices, said that the truth was more in line with the fact that Canada had found ways to control prescription drug prices as have most other countries. He stated that Americans are subsidizing the lower prices that Canadians and Europeans pay for pharmaceuticals. Waxman used the drug pricing problem to point out a need for a national health insurance system, like systems found in Canada and Europe that would help curb out-of-control drug costs.[10]

A final claim:

> **While prescription drugs are often blamed for rising healthcare costs, in fact they are one of the most dramatic ways to reduce costs.**

Rebuttal: There is evidence that many drugs have reduced or eliminated the need for longer hospital stays and some surgeries. However, the assertion that pharmaceutical products "are one of the most dramatic ways" to reduce costs is only true as long as the cost of the drug itself is affordable and that other avenues of care, including prevention are disregarded.

At the bottom of the ad the address for The Pharmaceutical Manufacturers Association in Washington D.C. appears with the note, "We would like to hear from you," and the tag line, "America's Research-Based Pharmaceutical Companies."

This statement is hotly contested by those who say that America's pharmaceutical companies are not researched-based, but instead are marketing based. For example, the

pharmaceutical publication, *The Pink Sheet,* published by
FDC Reports of Chevy Chase, Maryland, quotes a *New York
Times* article written by Elisabeth Rosenthal stating that
drug companies spent approximately $10 billion on promo-
tion in 1991 compared to $9 billion for research.

Actual promotion costs may be much higher, if it is true
as industry observers report, that it is typical for pharmaceutical companies to hide many promotional costs in categories such as "cost of sales," "other" or "miscellaneous."

As noted in Rosenthal's article, Dr. Stephen
Schondelmeyer (the University of Minnesota professor of
pharmaceutical economics) agrees. He suggests that the gap
between research and marketing is even greater, that the
average drug company spends 16 percent of its budget on
research and 20 percent on marketing.

Yet pharmaceutical companies complain that they don't
have enough money to invest in research.

Rosenthal writes that what research is being done is
often not geared toward ground-breaking innovation, but
toward "developing medicines that have the same function
as similar drugs made by rivals." This basically includes
drugs that have shown great profitability for their competitors. For example, of 90 new drugs approved in 1992,
fewer than 50 percent represented significantly new for-
mulations.

During his early days in office, President Clinton expressed concern for the high pricetag of promotion over research expenditures. Rosenthal notes that, "The industry
defends large marketing budgets on the grounds that at
least some of the promotion educates doctors and patients."

Rich Honey, a spokesman for Pfizer Inc., states that
because patent protection generally lapses in 10 to 15 years,
companies have only a few years to recoup expenses on
research. That reality, he says, justifies aggressive marketing.[11]

It seems to make good economic sense that in order to
survive, drug companies must reap profits while they can.
And profits they do reap. The following table shows annual
sales and net income based on four separate 12-month reports published in *Fortune* and *Forbes* magazines.[12, 13, 14, 15]

Annual Sales and Net Profits for Leading U.S. Pharmaceutical Manufacturers (in millions of dollars)

	1992	1993	1994	1995
Bristol-Meyers Squibb				
Sales	$11,805	$11,413	$11,984	$13,767
Net Profit	$1,962	$1,959	$1,842	$1,812
Merck				
Sales	$9,801	$10,498	$14,970	$16,681
Net Profit	$1,984	$2,166	$2,997	$3,335
Abbott Laboratories				
Sales	$7,894	$ 8,408	$9,156	$10,012
Net Profit	$1,239	$1,399	$1,517	$1,689
American Home Products				
Sales	$7,874	$8,305	$8,966	$13,376
Net Profit	$1,461	$1,469	$1,528	$1,680
Pfizer				
Sales	$7,415	$7,478	$8,281	$10,021
Net Profit	$811	$ 658	$1,298	$1,573
Eli Lilly				
Sales	$6,282	$6,452	$5,712	$6,764
Net Profit	$709	$480	$1,286	$2,291
Warner-Lambert				
Sales	$5,598	$5,794	$6,417	$7,040
Net Profit	$644	$ 331	$694	$739.5
American Cyanamid				
Sales	$5,348	$5,306		
Net Profit	$395	($1,119)		
Rhone-Poulenc Rorer				
Sales	$4,096	$4,019	$4,175	$5,142
Net Profit	$438	$ 409	$351	$357
Schering-Plough				
Sales	$4,094	$4,341	$4,657	$5,104
Net Profit	$720	$ 731	$ 922	$887
Upjohn				
Sales	$3,669	$3,611	$3,345	$7,095*
Net Profit	$324	$ 392	$491	$739*

*Pharmacia and Upjohn

Although *Forbes* reported that in 1993 the increased use of health maintenance organizations restricted pharmaceutical profits (Carol M. Cropper, "Health," *Forbes*,

January 3, 1994)[16], pharmaceutical sales still held the number one place among all major industries for median return on sales, return on assets and return on stockholders' equity and placed first by a substantial margin over the number two industry in all three categories for 1993 (*Fortune*, April 18, 1994, "Industry Overviews on The Fortune 500.")[17]

Financial Performance by Industry: Fortune 500 1993

Return on Sales	Return on Assets	Return on Stockholders' Equity
1. Pharmaceuticals 12.5%	Pharmaceuticals 11.2%	Pharmaceuticals 22.0%
2. Publishing/Prinitng 6.4%	Publishing/Printing 7.1%	Tobacco 16.5%
3. Electronics and Electronic Equipment 5.4%	Soaps, Cosmetics 6.9%	Beverages 15.1%

Rated among the top U.S. firms in the Forbes 500 Profits Rankings for 1994 were six pharmaceutical companies. Their profit ranking took on these characteristics that year.

Pharmaceutical Companies Ranking in Forbes 500 in 1994

Company	Net Profits*	Percent Change	Profit Ranking
Merck	$ 2,997	+ 38.4%	#10
Bristol-Myers Squibb	$ 1,842	- 6.0%	#22
American Home Products	$ 1,528	+ 4.0%	#31
Abbott Laboratories	$ 1,517	+ 8.4%	#32
Pfizer	$ 1,298	+ 97.5%	#39
Eli Lilly	$ 1,286	+161.9%	#41

in millions of dollars

In comparison, corporations ranked immediately after these pharmaceutical companies include Sears Roebuck, at #42 in net profits of $1,259 (in millions);

McDonalds, at #43, with $1,224.4 in net profits, and Walt Disney, at #44, with $1,224.2 in net profits.

Drug companies also rank among the most profitable industries in profits per employee. In the Forbes 500 rankings of productivity, the median profit per employee among all industries tracked in 1994 was $13,500. The Forbes 500 Health and Drugs category shows that these companies earned an industry median of $28,300 per employee. Taking the top ten companies in this category—not surprisingly, all drug companies—the median profit per employee rises to $44,300, more than three times or $30,800 per employee more than the Forbes 500 median. [18]

Finally, 1995 profit rankings and the percent of increase over the previous year listed in the Forbes 500: [19]

Pharmaceutical Companies Ranking in Forbes 500 in 1995—Profits Over $1 Billion

Company	Net Profits	Percent Change	Profit Ranking
Merck	$ 3,335	+ 11.3%	#9
Eli Lilly	$ 2,291	+78.1%	#21
Bristol-Myers Squibb	$ 1,812	- 1.6%	#33
Abbott Laboratories	$ 1,689	+ 11.3%	#36
American Home Products	$ 1,680	+10.0%	#37
Pfizer	$ 1,573	+ 21.1%	#39

(in millions of dollars)

With statistics demonstrating this level of profitability, the pharmaceutical industry has no apparent reason to claim it has inadequate dollars for research but must spend vast amounts to support marketing practices in order to be profitable.

David Kessler, commissioner of the FDA, told Rosenthal in her *New York Times* article that his concern about excessive marketing and promotional costs is not that it's wasteful, but that promotional techniques can be misleading and, consequently, dangerous. "Promotion is designed to create a market for a product, and the market created might not be the market that will benefit from the drug. So it's going to result in inappropriate prescribing, and people will be hurt," Kessler said.

Nowhere has truth in advertising been more of an issue than in the pharmaceutical industry, where marketing and public relations efforts have stretched the boundaries of ethical promotion.

In her book, *Disease Mongers*, Lynn Payer calls the process of exaggerating the severity of disease and making light of treatment (including the use of drugs) "disease mongering." She also labels as a disease-mongering tactic the implication in advertising that a normal function of the body should be treated; this is what social science would call, "medicalization." In this category, she includes so-called diseases such as PMS (pre-menstrual syndrome); childbirth and menopause.

Medicalization creates a market for its products by labeling the condition as something that needs treatment even when the conditions are a normal part of life and even though treating the condition with powerful drugs often causes more severe side effects than those of the condition itself.

Payer cites an effort by The Upjohn Company as case in point. The thirteenth largest U.S. pharmaceutical company at that time issued a press release on the signals of stress-related conditions. Physical and emotional symptoms included isolation, not taking time for one's self, job frustration and hostile or angry feelings. The release called for a visit to the doctor if these signals became persistent. Payer notes that most medical doctors are not trained to deal with emotional conditions and will usually prescribe a tranquilizer for lack of a better treatment. Undoubtedly, a tranquilizer made by Upjohn, perhaps one called Halcion, has as good a chance as any at being the prescribed treatment. Without mentioning its drug by name, the pharmaceutical house using this market technique creates demand and triggers orders.

Payer also notes that drug companies have a keen interest in creating the largest market possible for a disease and its treatment by obscuring the line between what is illness and what is not. This is especially common with "threshold diseases" such as hypertension and high cholesterol. By asserting that a diastolic level over the threshold of 90 rather than 95 is worth treating, the drug industry can dramatically increase the number of people needing treatment with hypertensive medications. Not surprisingly, Payer points out, a significant number of people have a diastolic reading between 90 and 95, but far fewer at more than 95.

Threshold diseases also give pharmaceutical companies a promotional edge since the news media are more eager to pick up a report if the illness affects a more significant portion of the population than if only a meager percentage or two are affected.[20]

In years past, the industry targeted MD's to get their message across, but when the FDA lifted its ban on advertising for prescription drugs, promoters saw their chance and ran with the ball toward their marketing goals.

A *Consumer Reports* article focusing on drug marketing accused the drug industry of banking on the idea that patients could persuade their doctors to write a prescription for the kind of drug they wanted, the one they had read about in a magazine, or the one they had seen work on television. The industry was also hoping to convince people to get their prescriptions filled because the one in three prescriptions being written by physicians that is never filled results in a loss of drug industry revenues to the tune of $1.2 billion. This kind of marketing turned the patient into a kind of associate doctor, the patient making suggestions and recommendations to the doctor based on information in paid messages from the pharmaceutical companies.

Eli Lilly's arthritis drug Oraflex was one of the first drugs to become a major media star. An antiinflammatory drug not significantly different from other similar drugs on the market, Oraflex was launched in a media campaign implying that Oraflex reversed the disease process of arthritis. The company sent a force of scientific experts throughout the country to promote its product and within six weeks, more than half a million arthritis-stricken people were taking the drug. Tragically, several deaths resulted from the drug's side effects, and the drug was removed from sale within three months of its release.[21]

Another Eli Lilly effort that came under fire in April of 1993 was the sponsorship of a promotional campaign designed to reach 93 percent of American adults. According to a *Wall Street Journal* article, Lilly paid between $3 and $4 million for a National Mental Health Association three-week blitz encouraging the public to seek professional help for depression. Lilly also gave the Virginia-based nonprofit organization $500,000 to conduct a nine-month public education program to identify potential candidates for treatment of depression. The "public service campaign" could be seen as merely an avenue to gain new patients for the drug Prozac, the world's best selling antidepressant drug, which is manufactured by Lilly. (Prozac is the controversial drug whose use has brought numerous claims that it can cause suicidal thoughts.)

The American Psychological Association pointed out that these public service ads direct people to consult their doctor if they believe they are suffering signs of depression. Psychologists, who generally can't prescribe medication, believe that this advice will lead people to their primary care physicians, who are most inclined to use medication rather than therapy as the sole treatment.

Lilly and the National Mental Health Association object to this criticism, contending that the ads were designed to encourage intervention, period—not just intervention with medication. The association points out that it endorses no product and that Lilly is not mentioned in the text of any of the ads, although it is credited for paying for the advertisements.

Eli Lilly defends its actions by saying that these kind of programs save lives and do not promote any one product. The mental health association agreed completely. Yet few would deny the actual interest of a profit-oriented organization with their involvement in such a campaign. This kind of action looks to many like another example of a profit motive masquerading as public interest without regard for health consequences.

Public Citizen Health Research Group adds that,
"The [Lilly] campaign is another example of pharmaceutical companies trying to influence patients' groups
through financial support." Sidney Wolfe who heads the
consumer advocacy group says that, "The money is given
to try to curry favor with groups so they don't resist or
oppose things happening with a drug. Or they become
de facto advocates for a drug."

Ronald Cann, senior vice president of medical affairs
at CMG Health of Owings Mills, Maryland., told the *Wall
Street Journal* that Prozac is already overprescribed.
Cann estimates the drug is appropriate for only one third
of the people it is now prescribed for. (CMG manages
mental health care plans for health maintenance organizations.)

Conveniently, the Agency for Health Care Policy and
Research (a federal agency) issued almost simultaneously
a release of a report to doctors advising more aggressive
diagnosis and treatment of depression.[22]

FDA regulations prohibit drug companies from promoting uses for products that it has not approved. The
regulatory agency also prohibits manufacturers from
concealing side effects. Nevertheless, sidestepping seems
to be the practice of preference. Much of this effort has
been done under the guise of public service and public
education pieces, often using noted figures who provide
testimonials.

For example, medical experts and celebrities often
sign contracts with drug companies to talk to groups of
doctors or the public armed with press kits and product
information. Those who listen to these spokespeople usually assume they are independent parties and have no
interest in the drug's promotion. In fact, a drug company has sponsored the person and is paying the celebrity well for pushing a product. Of even greater concern
is the fact that these "experts" often promote applications for drugs that still might be unapproved, a useful
approach since doctors are allowed to prescribe drugs
for uses still unapproved by the FDA.

Another tactic used by drug companies is to meet FDA requirements, but in a way that is often misleading or disguised. For example, the Sunday Lifetime Cable Channel runs special medical programs that are inseparable from drug ads. While the FDA requires a product promotion of its benefits to be balanced with information incorporating the drug's risks, ads appearing during the programming are not accompanied by complete product information. Instead, side effects and less positive information are often held until the end of the segment, appearing as a "credit," or, at best, information that seems to be less important because it appears incidentally at the end of the program.

The drug industry deserves high praise for their innovative marketing techniques but not for their ethical concerns. For example, drug companies have obtained patient databases to encourage brand loyalty. Names and addresses of patients have been used to mail prescription reminders to patients and build brand loyalty through these mailings.

Other techniques include setting up toll free numbers in media advertising so that patients can gain more information on specific drugs. Promotional pieces from drug companies in the form of video news releases (VNR's) save television stations production costs by simply using the video news pieces and splicing in their own journalists to give the coverage a local flavor and added credibility.

Drug companies have also manipulated information written for medical journals to their advantage. *Consumer Reports* noted a situation that involved Squibb capitalizing on a negative study in the *New England Journal of Medicine* suggesting that the use of diuretics (widely prescribed for high blood pressure) might increase the risk of heart attack.

The article's writers noted that the assertion was still speculative. Squibb responded to this report by stating that the risk of heart attack from the use of diuretics was a "near certainty" and recommended their own blood pressure medication, Capoten (captopril), a nondiuretic—

and a more expensive product. Following a high profile public relations campaign by Squibb, new prescriptions for diuretics dropped 13 percent. The sale of Capoten and similar drugs increased to fill the gap.

Drug interests have become skilled at circumventing FDA promotional restrictions that require full disclosure. Because of this, the FDA has issued new regulations including the requirement that VNR's must be submitted to them for review before they can be used. Also, the FDA has requested in a less forceful way, that press kits be cleared in advance. The degree of adherence to these guidelines is not known. Yet one fact remains: a large part of what we learn about health and about disease prevention comes not from independent researchers or medical professionals in the field, but from people whose major interest is in selling their own products.[23]

How successful is the marketing of pharmaceutical products? Pharmaceutical profits provide a clear idea of how successful this industry has been in their promotions to medical doctors and their patients. In 1983, retail sales of prescription drugs totaled $17 billion, according to the Pharmaceutical Manufacturers Association. Yet in 1993, the top 16 U.S. pharmaceutical companies alone (by gross sales of prescription and non-prescription drugs combined) pulled in more than $93 billion, with profits exceeding $11 billion, demonstrating the success of world class marketing.

Yet, with the increase in pharmaceutical drug use over the past decade, the question remains: "Is the public a healthier one?"

"No," say a growing number of industry critics who believe that the therapeutic benefits from drugs have not kept pace with sales.

Some may protest that these critics are misjudging the quality of medical care in the United States today. Yet, the facts show that we are dying faster than ever before from heart disease, cancer and a number of other diseases medical care has failed to control. Even though some medical proponents continue to argue successfully that medicine has extended the "quantity" of life to some degree, they cannot show that medicine has enhanced the "quality" of life. Length of life does not equate to quality of life—the two are only possible in tandem when a state of health exists. Medicine simply cannot deliver good health.

We might not mind watching drug companies and medical interests grow richer on our health dollar if only those dollars resulted in the public's increasing good health. Unfortunately, the only result is our collective poor health clearly reflecting our growing poverty.

1. "MD's Turn to PR to Improve Sagging Image," *The Chiropractic Journal,* August 1992.

2. "Why Unconventional Medicine?" editorial printed in *The New England Journal of Medicine,* Jan 28, 1993, by Edward W. Campion, MD

3. "Unconventional Medicine in the United States," *The New England Journal of Medicine,* Jan. 28, 1993, by David M. Eisenberg, MD,et al.

4. *Statistical Bulletin* (SB), published by Metropolitan Life, Volume 73, No. 3, July-September 1992.

5. *Public Citizen* (newsletter) Jan/Feb 1993.

6. "Day One," (television news magazine), October 18, 1993.

7. "Miracle Drug: Only $350,000 A Year," sidebar article written by Dick Thompson, *Time* magazine, Volume 141, No. 10, March 8, 1993.

8. "Ouch," article written by John Greenwald, *Time* magazine, Volume 141, No. 10, March 8, 1993.

9. "Merck Launches Campaign to Defend Drug Industry Prices," by AP Business Writer Mariann Caprino, reprinted in the *Kalamazoo Gazette* (MI), February 22, 1993.

10. "Drug Prices Sharply Lower in Canada," article by Milt Freudenheim, New York Times, reprinted in the *Kalamazoo Gazette* (MI), October 22, 1992.

11. "Drug Marketing Costs Exceed Research, Experts Say," article by Elisabeth Rosenthal of the *New York Times,* reprinted in the *Kalamazoo Gazette* (MI), February 22, 1993.

12. "The 500 By Industry," *Fortune,* April 19, 1993.

13. "The 500 Ranked Within Industries," *Fortune,* April 18, 1994.

14. "The Forbes Sales 500", and "The Forbes Profit 500," *Forbes,* April 24, 1995.

15. "The Forbes Sales 500" and "The Forbes Profit 500," *Forbes,* April 22, 1996.

16. "Health," *Forbes*, Carol M. Cropper, January 3, 1994.

17. "Industry Overviews on The Fortune 500," *Fortune,* April 18, 1994.

18. "The Forbes 500 Rankings, *Forbes,* April 24, 1995.

19. "The Forbes 500," *Forbes,* April 22, 1996.

20. Disease-Mongers, Lynn Payer, John Wiley & Sons: New York, 1992.

21. "Miracle Drugs or Media Drugs," *Consumer Reports*, March 1992, Volume 57, No.3.

22. "Critics See Self-Interest in Lilly's Funding of Ads Telling the Depressed to Get Help," *Wall Street Journal* (Marketplace), by Elyse Tanouye, April 15, 1993.

23." Miracle Drugs or Media Drugs," *Consumer Reports*, March 1992, Volume 57, No.3.

3

Drug Promises of Good Days and Sweet Nights

Controversy over the safety of prescription drugs remains a popular topic in the media. The continuous flow of stories on drug side effects has helped create a consciousness in the minds of the public who in increasing numbers is questioning the safety and efficacy of the prescriptions their doctors write for them. Allegations of the dangers of drug side effects range from claims of altered behavior to those claiming that a drug has been the causal factor in death.

As media coverage increases, concern over pharmaceutical products becomes more widespread. It is a sad commentary that the news media are more responsible for alerting the public of potential problems with drugs than the group that should be most responsible for the dissemination of information: physicians.

Yet, because media reports are often conflicting and flip-flop over time, these allegations ultimately create confusion. Fast-stepping drug manufacturers add to this confusion. The pattern is typical: first, a story appears linking a drug to serious side effects, then independent experts surface who agree with the drug's dangers. Their testimony encourages more stories relating to the drug's side effects. During this time, denials from the manufacturer enter the picture. As additional stories attesting to problems with the drug come to light, the pharmaceutical company firmly stands behind its product using expert testimony of researchers and medical practitioners to support the company's views.

With experts on both sides of the controversy asserting without a doubt that their own widely divided views are correct, the public is left with no where to turn except to their own doctors, who probably have no more information than the patient. Often, as in the cases of Prozac and Halcion, the manufacturers were able to construct substantial public relations campaigns. While the campaigns did not end up with full exoneration of their products, at least the drugs were saved from the chopping block. With billions of dollars at stake, the effort was worthwhile—for the drugs' manufacturers.

Eli Lilly's antidepressant Prozac brings in more than $1 billion in annual worldwide sales for its manufacturer. However, this highly prescribed drug has been reported to induce pronounced agitation and even violent tendencies in users, similar to symptoms related to the sleeping aid, Halcion, produced by the Upjohn company.

Even so, Prozac earned a reprieve in the fall of 1992 when the FDA ruled their own investigation did not find significant proof of the drug's dangers. Yet, the question exists: If Prozac did not cause compromising side effects, why were these claims being made? Critics of the drug say that the claims are in fact accurate, that this drug holds the potential to be highly dangerous. Yet, drug manufacturers are adept at overcoming virtually any barrier that stands in the way of sales, even barriers that allege a drug's side effects might include risk of death.

Eli Lilly overcame the major charges against Prozac, and for the most part, so have other companies with their own products including Upjohn and their highly profitable sleeping remedy, Halcion.

The world's most prescribed sleeping pill as of 1991 with sales that year of $237 million, Halcion gained worldwide attention when researchers claimed it held a lethal potential. According to a *Chicago Tribune* article, Anthony Kales, chairman of the Sleep Research Center at Penn State, petitioned the FDA in October of 1991 with his findings that people taking Halcion frequently suffered memory loss, confusion, hallucination and withdrawal symptoms in dosages that ranged from one quarter of a gram (or as low as one eighth of a gram, according to another article) to one milligram. He believed that there was an unacceptably high risk of serious side effects even at low dosages and that Halcion had a slim margin of safety when compared to other drugs in its class.

In the *Tribune* article, writer Michael Millenson noted that concern over the drug actually had begun much earlier in Europe. He wrote:

> Halcion was originally marketed in Europe in 1980
> in 1 milligram tablets, then was yanked from
> pharmacy shelves after a Dutch researcher
> reported the drug caused serious mental problems
> in some psychiatric patients. Upjohn challenged
> the data, and Dutch regulators allowed the drug to
> be remarketed in 1984 at the half-milligram dose.

Proponents of Halcion, including James Walsh, president of the American Sleep Disorders Association, see no significant difference between Halcion and other benzodiazepine drugs. In the *Tribune* article, Walsh asserted that all of Dr. Kales's concerns about the drug go back to the same 20 patients. Walsh adds, "There are literally dozens and dozens of other experiments from other laboratories which do not agree with [Dr. Kales's] papers."[1]

Yet there was evidence something was wrong. According to a December 1991 Associated Press piece, the FDA had knowledge of more than 2,000 cases with adverse reactions including approximately 50 homicides or attempted homicides since the drug was introduced in 1982.

Upjohn officials, including Dr. Geoffrey Jonas, a senior psychiatrist for the company, made the ludicrous claim that if Halcion were that dangerous, doctors wouldn't be prescribing it. The fact was that doctors evidently didn't know how dangerous Halcion might be.[2]

Although the company never wavered in its claims of Halcion's safety, Upjohn agreed to change the labeling information on the drug. The company notified doctors in late November of 1991 of new recommendations:

For most adults the dosage is adequate at 0.25 mg before bedtime.

A dosage of 0.125 mg is recommended for patients with low body weight.

A 0.5 mg dosage should be used only for exceptional patients who do not respond to a lower dose.

For geriatric and debilitated patients, the recommended dosage ranged from 0.125 mg to 0.25 mg. Specific recommendations were to initiate dosage at 0.125 for these patients, changing to 0.25 mg for patients not responding to a lower dose, with no dosage exceeding 0.25 for these patients.

A letter by Lawrence S. Olanoff, MD, Ph.D., and Corporate Vice President, Clinical Development and Medical Affairs for Upjohn, asserted in the revised recommendations that a dose of 0.5 mg should not be exceeded in any case. With this addendum, the revised maximum dose had been reduced by a full 50 percent from the earlier maximum of one milligram. In his letter, Dr. Olanoff stated that "the risk of adverse conditions increases with the size of the dose administered." The letter also stressed the point that Halcion was intended as a short-term treatment of insomnia (7-10 days), and that use for more than 2-3 weeks should include a complete reevaluation of the patient. Olanoff concluded the letter by saying, "As you are aware, Halcion is a safe and effective medication for the management of insomnia when used as directed."[3]

For Dr. Kales, whose research convinced him that Halcion was dangerous, changes in instruction weren't enough. He claimed that no alteration in dosage would make Halcion safe to use and adamantly asserted that Upjohn's concerns were mostly economic and that these should not take priority over consumer safety.[4] This economic concern seemed evident in the physician package insert where Upjohn downplayed serious side effects of the drug.

In this physician package insert, Upjohn pointed out that in addition to the expected sleepiness that might result, special concerns with benzodiazepine sleeping pills include dizziness, light-headedness and difficulty with coordination, but that these are expected as part of the drug reaction to make the patient sleep better.

Upjohn noted in the same revised package insert dated November 1991:

> All benzodiazepine sleeping pills can cause a special type of amnesia (memory loss) in which a person may not recall events occurring during some period of time, usually several hours, after taking a drug. This is ordinarily not a problem, because the person taking a sleeping pill intends to be asleep during this vulnerable period of time. It can be a problem when the drugs are taken to induce sleep while traveling, such as during an airplane flight, because the person may awake before the effect of the drug is gone. This has been called "traveler's amnesia." Halcion is more likely than other members of the class [benzodiazepine] to cause this problem.

Since amnesia is a possible side effect for the Halcion patient, a person using the drug could possibly forget having taken the tablet and then take another dosage. Since with Halcion the risk of serious side effects increases with the dosage taken, the chance of taking too large a dosage is a real possibility. The side effect of amnesia increases the potential of overdosing.

Upjohn admitted in its physician packaging notice:

> Some loss of effectiveness or adaptation to the sleep inducing effects of these medications [benzodiazepines] may develop after nightly use for more than a few weeks and there may be a degree of dependence that develops. For the benzodiazepine sleeping pills that are eliminated quickly from the body, a relative deficiency of the drug may occur at some point in the interval between each night's use. This can lead to (1) increased wakefulness during the last third of the

night, and (2) the appearance of increased signs of
daytime anxiety or nervousness. These two events
have been reported in particular for Halcion.

There can be more severe 'withdrawal' effects
when a benzodiazepine sleeping pill is stopped.
Such effects can occur after discontinuing these
drugs following use for only a week or two, but
may be more common and severe after longer
periods of continuous use. One type of withdrawal
phenomenon is the occurrence of what is known as
'rebound insomnia'. That is, on the first few nights
after the drug is stopped, insomnia is actually
worse than before the sleeping pill was given.
Other withdrawal phenomena following abrupt
stopping of benzodiazepine sleeping pills range
from mild unpleasant feelings to a major
withdrawal syndrome which may include
abdominal and muscle cramps, vomiting, sweating,
tremor, and rarely, convulsions. These more
severe withdrawal phenomena are uncommon.

The first paragraph points to the increased side effect
of wakefulness during the night with Halcion as well as
daytime anxiety after just a few weeks on the drug. Because of this, the potential for a patient taking more of the
drug to achieve relief from restlessness or anxiety and therefore exceeding the recommended dosage appears to increase
for those taking Halcion.

The second paragraph points to concerns addressing
the benzodiazepine class in general, and points to the serious side effects that may take place after only a short time
taking this category of medication, including Halcion as
well as others.

Another physician packaging directive read:

All benzodiazepine sleeping pills can cause
dependence (addiction) especially when used
regularly for more than a few weeks or at higher
doses. Some people develop a need to continue
taking these drugs, either at the prescribed dose
or at increasing doses, not so much for continued
therapeutic effect, but rather, to avoid withdrawal
phenomena and/or to achieve non-therapeutic

effects. Individuals who have been dependent on alcohol or other drugs may be at particular risk of becoming dependent on drugs in this class, but all people appear to be at some risk. This possibility must be considered before extending the use of these drugs for more than a few weeks.

And finally:

A variety of abnormal thinking and behavior changes have been reported to occur in association with the use of benzodiazepine sleeping pills. Some of these changes are like the release of inhibition seen in association with alcohol, e.g., aggressiveness and extroversion that seem out of character. Others, however, can be more unusual and more extreme, such as confusion, bizarre behavior, agitation, hallucinations, depersonalization, and worsening of depression, including suicidal thinking. It is rarely clear whether such events are induced by the drug being taken, are caused by some underlying illness or are simply spontaneous happenings. In fact, worsened insomnia may in some cases be associated with illnesses that were present before the medication was used. In any event, the most important fact is to understand that regardless of the cause, users of these medications should promptly report any mental or behavioral changes to their doctor.[5]

The admission that benzodiazepines, not just Halcion, may or may not contribute to mental and/or behavioral changes is well taken. Yet, the possibility alone that such a class of drugs could cause these problems might well deter potential takers of the product if all facts are disclosed to the patient not through package inserts alone, but through the patient's physician, a practice often neglected.

No matter what the possibilities, the assertion is clear that sleeping pills are powerful drugs that frequently cause side effects and that these drugs need to be taken with the greatest care. The strong possibility remains that those prescribed the drug might take it incorrectly, suffer serious side effects and experience addiction/withdrawal symptoms after taking the drug only a short period of time.

Considering the strong possibility of side effects as well as addiction when benzodiazepine drugs are used over an extended period of time, it is reasonable to question whether it is possible for a doctor to monitor a patient on the drug closely enough. This is a question that should be asked when any powerful drug is prescribed. Yet do doctors ask?

The general response from the medical community is that potential side effects of drugs such as benzodiazepine drugs are accepted as a part of the therapeutic risk. Still, researchers including Dr. Kales and a significant number of practitioners believe Halcion creates too great a risk, with the risks outweighing any possible benefit.

Upjohn's reaction to the allegations against Halcion was predictable. There was much at stake: the sales of Upjohn's second best selling drug, with annual sales of $237 million of the company's $3.4 billion in sales during 1991.[6]

Upjohn put an effective legal strategy into play by forcing those who had been on the offensive to go on the defensive. The company announced in January of 1992 that it planned to sue for libel. Their targets included Dr. Ian Oswald, a Scottish physician and critic of Halcion, for allegations he made that were printed in The New York Times.

A retired head of the department of psychiatry at the University of Edinburgh, Oswald had spent 30 years researching sleep. His work included studies using Halcion. After spending two years looking through Upjohn's data on the drug, Oswald concluded that "The whole thing has been one long fraud." He further accused Upjohn of covering up the truth about the side effects of Halcion that were much more dangerous than Upjohn claimed.

Gina Kolata of the New York Times reported that Oswald was called as an expert witness by an attorney who represented a Halcion user. Ilo Grundberg, a 57-year old Utah woman, killed her mother on the eve of her mother's 83rd birthday by shooting her eight times and then placing a birthday card in her mother's hand. The daughter used Halcion as her defense, saying that it made her psychotic. Murder charges against her were subsequently dropped and Upjohn settled a lawsuit with Grundberg for an unspecified amount just before that case was to be heard in court.

Upjohn settled to avoid an order to provide the plaintiff's attorneys with substantial new data on Halcion. (Initially, Upjohn wanted to block release of the information and obtained a court order to keep the data secret.) However, Upjohn wasn't as successful keeping the information from drug regulatory authorities, who decided to investigate. The major impact of the case and of Dr. Oswald's testimony was that the counterpart of the FDA in Britain decided to ban the drug saying that they probably would not have approved it had they known earlier what they learned from Oswald. Norway, Finland and Jamaica followed Britain's lead in banning Halcion.

Kolata reported in her *Times* article that another critic of Halcion, Dr. Graham Dukes, had also read excerpts of Upjohn's internal data. Dukes believed Upjohn minimized Halcion's side effects. A former medical director of the Dutch drug regulatory agency and later a professor of drug policy at Denmark's University of Gronigen, Dukes said that it was unlikely that Upjohn made simple errors in reporting their clinical findings. He contended that the clinical trials were so clear and so numerous that the true findings could not have been overlooked.

According to Kolata's article:

> In seeking FDA approval of Halcion, Upjohn submitted 87 studies, 34 of which lasted one week or longer. Upjohn's series of tests began in 1972 and continued even after the company obtained the necessary approval and began selling the drug in the United States in 1983.

> The problem with Halcion began, Oswald said, with the very first study, which took place in a Michigan prison. In that 1972 study, 28 subjects took 1-milligram Halcion tablets and 19 took a placebo. Seven of those taking Halcion had symptoms of paranoia, but Upjohn reported to the FDA that only two patients had such symptoms.

> The company also reported that two men taking the placebo in the prison study became paranoid, Oswald said, although in fact only one man did so. He said he discovered that Upjohn's analysts split

one man's side effect among two subjects. The FDA
was given the erroneous impression that Halcion
was no more likely than a placebo to cause
paranoia, he noted.

Oswald also pointed out that other Halcion studies were
altered in the final report to the FDA. One of the studies
involved testing 1,567 subjects with the drug where 188
patient cases were deleted from the study without the required explanation. The doctor also claimed that Upjohn
intentionally covered up reports of violent behavior in patients who were prescribed the drug by their doctors.[7]

Dr. William Barry, who directed Upjohn's
postmarketing-surveillance program from 1983 (when the
company began marketing Halcion) until just before he left
the company in 1990, also made clear to Upjohn officials
that by 1989 he was finding the same unsettling side effects. In a *Newsweek* magazine article, Geoffrey Cowley
reported that as early as 1983, Barry had written a company memo defining an unexpected number of amnesia com-
plaints from Halcion users.

In 1984, Barry realized from an in-house study that
patients on high doses were complaining of more amnesia,
confusion and hallucinations than patients on low doses.
He pointed out that a pattern like this wouldn't be found if
it weren't related to the drug. Barry sent memos to Upjohn
officials urging them to provide stronger warnings of the
drug's potential effects which included paranoia, psychosis
and homicidal behavior.

Upjohn shrugged off Barry's findings saying that they
were similar to what the FDA had already found and that
there was no need for further action. In turn, a company
spokesperson said that anecdotal reports were not valid in
determining specific frequency of reactions. Barry agreed,
but the lack of action by Upjohn after the findings he
brought to their attention seemed to demonstrate a lack of
concern that led to the cover-up of a study linking prolonged
Halcion use to extreme daytime anxiety. Upjohn's general
apathy toward any and all negative findings regarding
Halcion use seemed to become a kind of "company policy,"
according to Cowley.[8]

Yet another problem with Halcion research included Protocol 6045, four 28-day studies of 129 actual insomniacs in a clinical trial of the drug. *Newsweek* magazine brought their findings to the attention of the FDA reporting that the doctor who enrolled, treated and examined the subjects in the Protocol 6045 study had confessed fraud. Dr. William C. Franklin, an internist at the Clinic of the Southwest in Houston, assisted pharmaceutical companies in testing new products during the 1960s and 1970s. According to Geoffrey Cowley's *Newsweek* article, Dr. Franklin was exposed in an FDA investigation to have "fabricated patient records and failed to report adverse reaction in several drug studies."

Dr. Franklin was not accused of wrongdoing in the Halcion study, but he agreed not to participate in any new pharmaceutical product investigations.

Because of Dr. Franklin's activities, the FDA notified Upjohn that any study involving him could not be submitted in support of claims for Upjohn's product. Upjohn responded by saying that Dr. Franklin's role in Halcion studies was negligible. The company did not report that Dr. Franklin participated in Protocol 6045, the largest of the three pivotal studies on Halcion and minimized his work on the second largest Halcion study, Protocol 6041, saying that it was "unlikely that the deletion of his data would have a meaningful impact on the overall incidence of reactions."

Even with the information on Dr. Franklin out in the open, Upjohn continued to deny any wrongdoing.[9]

The late Dr. Theodore Cooper, chief executive officer of the Upjohn company during the Halcion controversy, attempted to soften the allegations by admitting that the company may have made "a few errors" in their reports to the FDA, but that Halcion was no more dangerous than any other sleeping pill in its class.[10]

Many users strongly disagreed with Dr. Cooper. These users included author William Styron who chronicled the dangers of Halcion he himself experienced. In his book *Darkness Visible: A Memoir of Madness*, Styron wrote that Halcion was at least the cause of exaggerating his own suicidal tendencies, tendencies that disappeared when his doctor took him off the drug.

In Styron's article "Prozac Days, Halcion Nights," published in *The Nation,* January 4/11, 1993, the writer notes that after his book was published,

> I was stunned by the volume of mail I received,
> but nothing impressed me more than the large
> number of correspondents—I would estimate
> perhaps 15 or 20 percent—who spoke of their own
> Halcion-induced horrors, homicidal fantasies,
> near-suicides and other psychic convulsions.

In letters to Styron, people also spoke of their own experiences with Prozac. The author states:

> What is distressing is the fact that a significant
> number of people do have very bad reactions to
> Prozac, chiefly suicidal impulses (the letters to me
> reflect this), and it is Lilly's concerted efforts to
> minimize such sinister side effects that remain
> even now indefensible.[11]

In an earlier article published in *The Nation*, Alexander Cockburn pointed out that Lilly used the counterattack approach with Prozac, forcing those initially on the offensive to become defensive, just as Upjohn did with selected critics of Halcion. Lilly turned the news media on to a major Prozac critic: the Church of Scientology. When the Church of Scientology made a public outcry against Prozac because of its potential for side effects, Lilly countered by encouraging the media to look into Scientology. The result was a discrediting of the church, which diminished both the church's public image and their allegations over Prozac.

During this debate, the FDA initiated a study of Prozac, yet as Cockburn pointed out, five of the study committee's eight members had financial backing from Lilly and in the end gave Prozac the go-ahead.[12]

Styron underscored an important point about mood-altering legal drugs:

> Tranquilizers [such as Halcion] should not be
> confused with antidepressants [such as Prozac],
> although [tranquilizers] are often prescribed to
> sedate people with depression. I wanted to point

> out that my own bleak experience had convinced me that virtually all the commonly prescribed minor tranquilizers (also known as benzodiazepines) are of questionable value even for healthy people; for those suffering from depression they should be shunned like cyanide, and of them all the most indisputably monstrous is a tiny gray-green oval called triazolam, better known by the brand name Halcion.

Styron went on to say that his depression was not directly caused by Halcion but that he was convinced the drug greatly exaggerated his illness by intensifying his suicidal thoughts and forcing hospitalization.

While he believes that Lilly used questionable tactics to lend support to its product, Styron states that Prozac does seem to be an effective antidepressant for many people. The fact that Lilly admits to no deficiencies with their product led Styron to believe that the company is no more ethical than any other huckster when it comes to selling.

Styron gave no such leeway to Upjohn whom he believes to be the "Crazy Eddie" of the pharmaceutical industry, promoting its products with what he labels "disgraceful hype."[13]

In another well-noted case, *Newsweek* reported that Jeffrey Dahmer, who pleaded guilty but insane to murdering 15 young men in Milwaukee, gave his victims Halcion. One of the victims reported that he had felt ill after having a drink with Dahmer. Another reported having passed out, waking up at a hospital the next day.[14]

One of many lawsuits with Halcion as the focus came out of Kentucky where a woman sued Upjohn claiming her husband committed suicide while taking the drug. The woman, Mary Ann Johnson, contended that Upjohn hid information about Halcion's side effects from the FDA.

According to an Associated Press article in January of 1992, Mrs. Johnson watched her husband's personality change once he started taking Halcion. For example, he believed the CIA was trying to eavesdrop on him by means of an intravenous needle. Mr. Johnson had also been hospitalized for a loss of balance, a recognized side effect of Halcion.[15]

Halcion made the news again when former president George Bush apparently experienced ill effects including mood swings and confusing language after taking the drug. The President referred to the Nitty Gritty Dirt Band as the Nitty Ditty Nitty Gritty Great Bird. Dr. Sidney Wolfe, director of Public Citizen's Health Research Group, part of the consumer advocacy group created by Ralph Nader, was quoted in a *Miami Herald* article saying, "The drug is not consistent with responsible governing of the nation, a state, a city or any other body."

According to the *Herald* article February 2, of 1992, "Wolfe's group has worked for years to force Halcion's manufacturer, The Upjohn Co., to more fully advise doctors and patients of the drug's side effects."

At the height of the controversy in early 1992, Upjohn announced that the company would defend doctors who prescribed Halcion and then were sued by patients. Their message appeared to be, "Go ahead. Prescribe Halcion even if it is dangerous. We'll protect you." The move took the responsibility off the most crucial checkpoint between the manufacturer and the patient—the doctor, whose responsibility should ultimately be aligned with patient welfare instead of with pharmaceutical interests, in this case Upjohn's financial power.

Benjamin Stein, a former speech writer for Richard Nixon, said he himself had taken many prescription drugs including Halcion and said that Halcion was the most "terrifying drug I have ever used." A report in *The New York Times* in early 1992 quoted Stein saying, "Its effects are incalculably more frightening when they are at work on the president..."[16]

A Grand Rapids, Michigan, personal injury attorney announced in February of 1992 that he was preparing between 30 and 50 suits against Upjohn representing clients from around the country. Attorney Joseph William Moch stated that Halcion was a dangerous drug with horrendous side effects.

By June of 1993, Moch acknowledged that there had been little progress with suits against Upjohn since the company's strategy of appealing to higher courts each time a judgment is made for a plaintiff has been successful.

"Upjohn believes they have the resources including time and money to outlast those who challenge the safety of Halcion," Moch said, noting that the strategy is not used exclusively by the pharmaceutical industry, but by big business in general.

Pointing the finger should not be directed at Upjohn alone. Blame should weigh heavily on the FDA, the attorney declared. "The government and its agencies have done next to nothing to correct problems like Halcion. They simply grease the skids for approval." Moch accused the government of only pretending to monitor and control industry activities. "There's a need for regulation. Because if big business can get away with it, of course they will." Moch said that ironically he probably has more information on the drug Halcion than the FDA, an illustration of either the FDA's inability to handle such issues or the low priority drug safety occupies.

Moch also finds the judicial system to be at fault. He noted one Halcion suit, Petty v. Upjohn, in which the presiding judge cited Moch for inadvertently adding an extra "s" to the word "business" in documents submitted to the court. The judge's penalty resulted in an indefinite postponement of the case. "It's frightening that people in positions like this can be in the back pocket of big business," Moch alleges. He supports his suspicion by noting that Petty v. Upjohn was heard in a Kalamazoo, Michigan court, the same city many Upjohn family members call home.

> "There's a need for evenness. There's a need for fairness, and the last bastion of fairness in the courtroom seems to come by way of the jury trial. Even so, today, there is a movement sponsored in large part by corporate entities to eliminate trial by jury, which would leave cases to be decided exclusively by judges. If the judicial systems seems unfair now, just wait until this happens," Moch said.

Moch pointed out that although Halcion is a dangerous drug, the pharmaceutical product he believes will make Halcion pale in comparison is one called Depo Medrol, now on the market. A synthetic antiinflammatory, the drug has been shown to cause a number of severe side effects including paralysis.

In 1991, a jury awarded an Illinois man one of the largest personal injury awards in U.S. history—$128 million after he lost an eye his doctor had injected with Depo Medrol. The jury decided on $3 million in compensatory damages and approximately $124.6 million in punitive damages against the manufacturer. The plaintiff's attorney had accused the manufacturer of callous marketing tactics.[17]

According to Moch, side effects of Depo Medrol were reported in Australian studies to adversely affect up to 17 of every 20 people taking the drug. The drug is an Upjohn product.

"The only good that has come so far from controversial drugs that have been well-noted in the media is that doctors are sitting up and taking notice," Moch said. From what he has seen, the attorney feels Upjohn's own Halcion studies were simply inaccurate. Some studies were nonexistent. Others were tampered with to reach the desired outcome. Moch believes a doctor must weigh all the information to decide whether a drug like Halcion is worth the risk and if it is prescribed, that doctor has an obligation to monitor the patient closely for adverse side effects.[18]

The arguments and actions both for and against Halcion have continued throughout the controversy, each one contradicting the last. These include the following:

A European Government Medical Organization's Pro-Halcion Argument—The European Community's Committee for Proprietary Medicinal Products agreed with the statement that an insignificant number of people suffer ill side effects from the drug. After investigating the sleeping pill, they gave it their okay for short-term use while commending the company for revising packaging instruction and downsizing dosages.[19]

One Government's Action Against Halcion—During the summer of 1993, the British Government upheld its ban of Halcion and withdrew the drug's license.[20]

A Pro-Halcion Argument, But With a Disclaimer—Mitchell Balter, a private researcher, formerly of the National Institute of Mental Health, was quoted in a *Chicago Tribune* story saying that he found no greater occurrence of side effects in Halcion than with other benzodiazepines.

He did say, however, that his survey relies on people re-calling reactions to a drug they took during the past year, a less reliable method than ongoing studies.[21]

Upjohn's Pro-Halcion Argument—An Upjohn spokeswoman told the *Miami Herald* that Halcion was "safe and effective when used appropriately." Kaye Bennett added, "One of the advantages is that it's short acting. It puts you to sleep quickly and clears your system quickly." But in the same article, the *Herald* pointed out that, "Although drowsiness brought on by Halcion can wear off after five hours, its side effects can persist into the next day. These can include amnesia, confusion, anxiety, hostility, hallucinations, agitation and, in very rare cases, violence."[22] The "short acting" element appears to be yet another element open to individual interpretation.

A Psychiatrist's Argument for General Caution: In a May 9, 1992 *Chicago Tribune* article, Dr. Stuart Yudofsky, chairman of psychiatry at Houston's Baylor College of Medicine and author of a well-known guide to psychiatric drugs said that, "Any medication is dangerous if not used correctly...People tend to be maintained on these medications more than they should be and prescriptions are filled again and again without medical monitoring." Yudofsky nevertheless did criticize Upjohn for originally marketing Halcion at too high a dosage.[23]

Beyond Halcion, Upjohn's alleged lack of public concern over product safety arose with yet another of their drugs in the benzodiazepine class—Xanax—the company's best selling product. It, too, came under fire on two different fronts in 1992 and 1993.[24]

In an issue of *Consumer Reports*, Xanax was called an ineffective and addictive drug. The magazine said that Upjohn misled doctors into believing Xanax was more therapeutic than it really was by highlighting a particular section of a phase-one research study. Upjohn touted a stronger response of patients to the anti-anxiety medication than to those in the study taking a placebo. Yet, at the conclusion of the study, there was no apparent difference between the two groups.

The article also noted that patients who had taken Xanax could become dependent on it after only a few weeks.

Of John Hopkins researchers specializing in helping patients withdraw from benzodiazepines, 84 percent said that
Xanax was an especially difficult drug to withdraw from.
Only 29 percent of the researchers answered the same question by naming Valium.[25]

Xanax also found a place in the news when critics compared costs of drugs in the United States to those in Canada.
The 1991 wholesale price in Canada was $16.92 for 100
tablets while the price in the U.S. was $47.81 for the same
number of pills. *Time* magazine (March 8, 1993) noted that
the price of Xanax in the United States increased by 87.4
percent from 1987 to 1992.[26]

Author William Styron attacks Xanax, as well as
Halcion and Prozac. He accuses Upjohn of disgraceful "snake
oil" marketing in its promotion of Xanax and refers to another critical article written by Cynthia Cotts for *The Nation*. Styron writes that Upjohn has been responsible for
promoting Xanax as if it were as harmless as Gatorade. If
there is a continuum from ethical to non-ethical pharmaceutical companies, his sources say that Merck is often mentioned with reverence. On the low end, he names Upjohn.

Because of his background with Xanax, Halcion and
Prozac, Styron has frequently been asked to speak about
his experience and knowledge of the drugs.

One occasion brought him to a psychiatric conference
where he was to speak before an audience of approximately
30 journalists. During this meeting, a reporter asked him
for his opinion concerning Prozac. Styron responded by saying that although he had never used it personally, he had
mixed feelings—that for some it was apparently beneficial,
while for others it seemed to do little at all. For a certain
group of users, he said, Prozac seemed to produce extreme
side effects, primarily suicidal fantasies. Although he tried
to continue, he was courteously pushed to the side by the
director of the National Institute of Mental Health who
claimed that (according to Styron's *The Nation* article):

> **Every medication has unpredictable side-**
> **effects...but it has been clearly determined that**
> **Prozac is virtually free of the serious reactions**
> **that have plagued antidepressants in the past. No**
> **safer and more reliable treatment for depression**

has ever been available to therapists and
physicians—a truly remarkable development in
psychopharmacology. Any more questions?

There were more questions from reporters, but none
were directed to Mr. Styron. Instead the audience was
treated to a glowing portrayal of Prozac from the institute
director. Styron noted that the conference was sponsored
by Eli Lilly.

As Styron left the speaker's platform, a sympathetic
journalist said to him, "Boy, the guv'ment sure did shut
you up, didn't they?"[27]

Yet, with all the information available on the dangers
of drugs such as Prozac, Xanax and Halcion, doctors and
patients alike remain loyal to these drugs, with the exception of Halcion.

Prozac, the most popular of the three drugs, has gained
public confidence. In 1992, Prozac ranked as the #17 best-
selling drug in U.S. community pharmacies. In 1993, it became the #16 best selling drug. By 1994, it was in the top
ten best-selling drugs at #10, and in 1995, it had gained
another rung at #9. Although, as Styron said, the antidepressant seems to help a number of people, the concern is
for those who are taking the drug who shouldn't be, who at
any time may experience the drug's potential of inducing
suicidal induced impulses. This potentially deadly product
is the ninth best-selling drug sold in U.S. pharmacies.

Xanax dropped from the #7 position in 1992 and 1993,
to #28 in 1994 and #70 in 1995. However, the primary reason Xanax has fallen from use is that Upjohn's patent protection of the drug was lost in 1993. Other generic drugs of
its kind have taken over a solid share of the market.

As for Halcion, by the early 1990s sales were reflecting
the damage created by the media's negative reports. In 1992,
Halcion ranked as the #81 best selling drug in U.S. pharmacies. From there, Halcion fell to #110 in 1993 and then
off the list of the top #200 drugs in 1994.[28]

Today, the word "Halcion" incites fear in those who have
heard the media reports and listened to the stories of alleged homicidal and suicidal tendencies the drug is thought
to cause. *En masse*, doctors and patients alike have

heeded the warnings and elected other forms of benzodi-azepines or other avenues of care.

To critics of the pharmaceutical industry, it is only unfortunate that the names of more drugs fail to instill the kind of fear the name "Halcion" does. It is only unfortunate that the news media neglects the tens of other drugs that also hold the potential of life-shattering side effects.

1. "Upjohn Hit by Debate On Halcion," Michael Millenson, *The Chicago Tribune.* March 9, 1992.

2. Associated Press, December 9, 1991, (printed in the *Kalamazoo Gazette*, December 9, 1991).

3. Letter to Prescribing Doctors, issued by Lawrence Olanoff, MD, Ph.D., The Upjohn Company, November 22, 1991.

4. Associated Press, December 9, 1991.

5. Revised Information For The Patient About Halcion, November 1991, issued by The Upjohn Company.

6. "New Halcion Suit Seeks $63 Million," Lynn Turner, *Kalamazoo Gazette*, February 19, 1992.

7. "Critics Reiterate Claims Upjohn...." *The New York Times, Gina* Kolata, (printed in the Kalamazoo Gazette, January 20, 1992).

8. "Fueling the Fire Over Halcion," by Geoffrey Cowley, *Newsweek,* May 25, 1992.

9. "Another Questionable Doctor Tested Halcion, *Newsweek* Says," Geoffrey Cowley, *Newsweek,* (appearing in the Kalamazoo Gazette, February 11, 1992).

10. Kolata, *New York Times,* (printed in the *Kalamazoo Gazette,* January 20, 1992).

11. "Prozac Days, Halcion Nights," William Styron, *The Nation,* January 4/11, 1993.

12. "Beat The Devil," Alexander Cockburn, *The Nation*, December 7, 1992.

13. Styron, *The Nation,* January 4, 1993.

14. "Halcion & Jeffrey Dahmer," (excerpt taken from Newsweek), *Kalamazoo Gazette,* February 9, 1992.

15. "Kentucky Widow Files New Halcion Lawsuit," (printed in the *Kalamazoo Gazette,* January 31, 1992), Associated Press.

16. "Bush's Use of Sleeping Pill Questioned," *The Miami Herald*, February 2, 1992, Martin Merzer.

17. *Business Insurance News,* Meg Fletcher, October 28, 1991.

18. Author interview with Joseph Moch, attorney, Grand Rapids, Michigan, 1993.

19. *Kalamazoo Gazette*, December 29, 1991.

20. *Wall Street Journal,* June 10, 1993.

21. *Chicago Tribune,* March 9, 1992, Millenson.

22. *The Miami Herald,* February 2, 1992. Merzer.

23. *The Chicago Tribune,* March 9, 1992. Millenson.

24. "Consumer Reports Calls Xanax Ineffective," Lynn Turner, *Kalamazoo Gazette*, December 22, 1992.

25. *Consumer Reports,* January 1993.

26. *Time Magazine,* March 8, 1993, "Ouch!" John Greenwald.

27. *The Nation*, January 4, 1993, Styron.

28. "Drugs Dispensed Most Often In U.S. Pharmacies," *American Druggist,* February 1994, Pg. 28; February 1995, Pg. 21; and February 1996, pg. 19.

4

To Invade Illness, Not Prevent It

"For the sick, the least is best."—Hippocrates

From birth through death, Americans are conditioned to accept and fit into the channels medicine has created, a maze designed to ensure the greatest invasiveness in patient treatment and consequently, the most profitability for those who serve as its engineers and carry out the processes. People are not told how to prevent illness for the most part, just how they should obtain treatment once they are sick, once they are diseased.

Of course there are public education campaigns with the goal of encouraging people to exercise

more, eat less saturated fat and reduce cholesterol
intake, and then encouragement to eat more fiber
and whole grains, fruits and vegetables. But
beyond that, medicine is best at one thing—
treating the sick and dying, not preventing people
from getting sick in the first place. The medical
profession, for the most part, discourages people
from pursuing avenues that are based on
prevention—holistic or alternative health care
methods—saying that they are nothing more than
a waste of money—quackery. Yet a majority of the
treatments medicine uses are not proven in a way
the medical field would like the public to believe
they have been. So, doesn't it make sense that the
medical community continues to promote
expensive ineffective treatment that perpetuates
care and at the same time, denies the effectiveness
of alternative and preventive care especially when
there is so much money to be made treating the
sick and dying?—Dr. Michael Epitropoulos, D.C.,
Chiropractor/Nutritionist

This opinion, expressed by a majority of practitioners
of nontraditional healthcare, is also shared, if only in part,
by many in the medical profession itself including Alexander
Leaf, MD, whose article "Preventive Medicine for Our Ailing Health Care System," appeared in the *Journal of the
American Medical Association.* Dr. Leaf writes,

Medicine traditionally stands on two pillars:
prevention and cure. For the past century this
profession has rallied almost exclusively under the
banner of curative medicine. Preventive medicine
has been largely relegated to the Public Health
Service. Medical education provides minimal time
and instruction in preventive medicine. Third-
party insurers eschew payments for preventive
interventions, as is the case of Medicare, or
skimpily support secondary or tertiary preventive
measures. I think any impartial examination of the
evidence would indicate the need for a major
change in the emphasis.

Dr. Leaf cites heart disease as an example. He observed that in 1993, an estimated 1.5 million Americans
would suffer a myocardial infarction and one third
(500,000) of these victims would die, 300,000 before

reaching a hospital. Cardiovascular disease was estimated to cost $108.9 billion in 1992. Based on these statistics, Leaf identifies the downfall of the curative approach at three levels. First, once the victim has suffered a heart attack, chances are slim that he or she will reach treatment in time. Second, the number of people treated with coronary artery bypass grafts or other surgical measures only scratches the surface of those who might benefit with surgery, and if all those who needed treatment attempted to access it, trained personnel, facilities and dollars would be inadequate. Third, with all the technology available including drugs and surgery, "none do anything about the underlying atherosclerotic disease that causes the problem."

Perhaps the most significant failing of the curative approach, says Leaf, is that intervention once the disease has taken hold does nothing for the generations who will follow, those destined to repeat the same dismal statistics.

The JAMA article notes that "From 1978 to 1988, there was a 29.2 percent reduction in the age-adjusted death rate from heart attacks in the United States. " But Leaf points out that the improvement comes from people adopting healthier lifestyles, not from medical treatments. Healthier lifestyles are an example of the preventive, rather than the curative approach.

Leaf's article mentions that lifestyle changes alone—without medication—have been shown to create improvement even in individuals with advanced coronary heart disease. These lifestyle changes include programs that reduce risk factors and improve physical fitness.

Although programs such as cardiac rehabilitation exist, Leaf believes most physicians are unaware of the benefits associated with them. Instead, the majority of physicians continue to rely on drugs and surgery as the avenue of choice. Most ironic is that insurance companies turn a blind eye on prevention. Although Blue Cross/Blue Shield and Medicare will pay tens of thousands for coronary bypass graft operations and hundreds of thousands for heart transplant surgery, they won't consider covering the costs of a $1000-$2000 rehabilitation program. Medicare specifically eschews reimbursement for preventive measures.

A major obstacle in implementing preventive programs is an absence of cost benefit analyses. Leaf says that these analyses have not yet established that preventive care will save dollars and lives. After all, he notes, how do you assign a dollar value to health and quality of life?

Yet, he says, "I think there is much to indicate that a health care system, the goal of which is to prevent illness and to promote health, will cost less than the present system that basically operates to respond to the presence of illness, often with very costly diagnostic and therapeutic interventions."

Leaf does not diminish the advances in diagnostic and therapeutic methods because he believes there will always be those who for genetic or other reasons will develop disease even with preventive measures, but the saddest part of medicine, he says, is the incredible number of people who seek medical treatment for illnesses that could have been prevented. "We need to establish a balance between the 'curative' and preventive approaches." He realizes that this balance can only be achieved through major cultural changes in the medical community and the public, a type of reconditioning of attitudes toward health and disease.

Part of this change will come as the public accepts more responsibility for their own health, including lifestyle changes and obtaining information on the care choices available rather than relying entirely on their doctors and insurance companies to make that decision. "[People] will need to be disabused of the fantasy that they can indulge in whatever life-style they wish and that, when illness strikes, medicine will make available a pill or operation to erase the adverse health effects of a lifetime of self-abuse." Leaf asserts that physicians need to take responsibility in helping to create this revised approach to healthcare.

Leaf places blame for the excessive drugs and surgery route on the government and third-party medical insurers who reimburse specialists, i.e., cardiologists, radiologists, surgeons, etc., at many times the remuneration of general physicians. It is largely because of this imbalance— where invasive procedure pays and prevention does not—that drugs and surgery become the chosen method of care.

It is generally a myth that doctors are doctors because they want to be involved totally in healing. The medical community as a whole is as market-driven as any other business or profession. If surgery pays more than prevention, if a cardiologist makes more than a rehabilitation-focused physician, it's easy to see where the career choice will lie.[1]

The late Robert Mendelsohn, MD, and author of the book *Male Practice* and *Confessions of a Medical Heretic*, served as a major critic of the institution of modern medicine for more than thirty years. His argument with medicine spans the spectrum of care from the profession's monopoly of the birth process to the manner in which it handles the ill and aged.

Mendelsohn strongly believed that medicine is invasive before it is anything else. He watched a profession that changed pregnancy, a "normal physiological process," into a "life-threatening nine-month disease." He asserted that the medical community promotes pregnancy as if it were something to be remedied, the best approach to encourage more tests and additional procedures. Mendelsohn was convinced that unnecessary intervention caused the most complications during birth.

Some of Dr. Mendelsohn's views on how medicine treats pregnancy as a disease:

Most obstetricians encourage weight management during pregnancy. Yet weight management is dangerous when a woman tries to comply with her doctor's expectations. Basically, it's not the amount of weight the mother gains during her pregnancy, he said, but the quality of food she eats. If a baby is born with low birth weight, the chance of death in the first month of birth is greatly increased.

Mendelsohn also writes that although practitioners are more hesitant when pregnancy is involved, doctors are often too quick and too careless in prescribing prescription or over-the-counter drugs for pregnant women. When a woman experiences, for example, edema or fluid retention (in most cases, a normal part of pregnancy), medicine prescribes diuretics (with the encouragement of drug company promotions), rather than opt for the non-invasive approach of correcting diet and nutrient intake. The result of diuretics

can be devastating. Mendelsohn notes that these drugs increase nutrient loss in the body which can be dangerous for
both the mother and her child. Diuretics can also cause
other complications.

Morning sickness is another example of a condition
medicine often treats as a disease. One third to one half of
all pregnant women experience morning sickness, and
nearly as many suffer from heartburn. Doctors often encourage their patients to take antacids or prescribe medication to relieve stomach distress. Mendelsohn stated that,
"There is ample evidence that some drugs taken by the
mother during early months of pregnancy can cross the
placental barrier and damage the fetus...The hazards are
sufficiently grave that no doctor should prescribe any drug
for pregnant women unless he has a lifesaving reason for
doing so."

Mendelsohn believes that the worst step for the mater-
nity patient began when medicine replaced the midwife. This
was achieved by "interfering with the natural process and
creating medical interventions that only [doctors] could perform."

Mendelsohn asserts that medicine has captured the
birthing process by insisting on unnatural and even dangerous methods.

In the first place, women are placed on their backs
to deliver and are often on their backs from the time
they enter the hospital. With no help from gravity, this
almost assures that a birth requires a doctor's assistance.
"The supine lithotomy [on the back] position is the basis
for most of the intervention that is routine in most ob-
stetrical practice," Mendelsohn states.

Mendelsohn cites a survey conducted in 1933 by the
team Mengert and Murphy who recorded intra-abdominal
pressure at the height of straining during labor. It was found
that the greatest pressure could be exerted in the sitting or
squatting position since this alters the pelvic area in a way
that encourages delivery. Another study in 1937 concurred.
Yet today, women often give birth with their feet in stir-
rups while positioned flat on their backs.

Drugs are often introduced for pain as well as to expedite labor, and IVs are often introduced containing nutri-

ents and fluids; these change the entire process from natural to surgical. Fetal monitors are strapped on to the mother's stomach or inserted internally to measure fetal activity. All invasive procedures, including monitoring efforts, can create fetal trauma, and some of the methods can create infections and other medical problems, Mendelsohn reported.

An episiotomy, an incision to enlarge the vaginal opening, is performed in 80 to 90 percent of first births and in 50 percent of later births, according to the text *What to Expect When You're Expecting.* Birthing centers, which regularly involve nurse/midwives, hold a striking contrast in statistics where only 15 to 25 percent of births involve episiotomies. In birthing centers an additional 25 to 30 percent of women experience some tearing requiring repair. However, proponents of natural birth usually agree that minor tearing is better than incision.

Cesarean sections are performed too often on too many women, Dr. Mendelsohn stated, instead of waiting for the natural process of birth to take place. Medical doctors say they opt for C-section births when any risk to the mother or child is indicated. Yet, natural birth advocates agree with Mendelsohn, saying that C-sections are more desirable to the doctors who perform them than to the mothers and children who should be the ultimate consideration. For example, a midwife will allow the time necessary for the birth process to take place, while doctors often work to expedite the process. Consequently, midwife-directed births have a lower incidence of invasiveness.[2]

Hospitals generally have a C-section rate of 30 to 50 percent. Compare this to the Michigan Midwives Association statistics for 1988. With 552 attempted home births, only 20, or 3.6 percent, required transportation to the hospital for C-section delivery. For those who advocate home- or nurse/midwife rather than doctor-directed births, statistics speak for themselves. What they say is that when medicine is involved, invasiveness and complicated procedures are the methods of choice.[3]

Natural birth advocates also find it ironic that for thousands of years the vast majority of births have taken place in the home with few or no complications. When it comes to hospital births, by contrast, complications seem to be the norm rather than the exception.

Other critics of medical intervention include the late Adelle Davis, one of the country's leading nutritionists, whose books *Let's Have Healthy Children* and *Let's Get Well*, point to the dangers of medical procedures during the prenatal months and throughout life. In *Let's Have Healthy Children*, Davis notes that the most common accidental poisoning comes from taking aspirin, and that approximately 15 percent of accidental poisoning deaths in young children are caused by aspirin. Yet millions of dollars are spent annually on "baby" aspirin.

Davis points out that many drugs deplete vitamins in the body. Aspirin reduces blood platelet and plasma levels of vitamin C. Drugs including penicillin and other antibiotics can deplete Vitamin B6, and Vitamin K levels to the point that convulsion, hemorrhaging and other abnormalities, not excluding juvenile diabetes, can result. Many drugs, including antibiotics, can cause liver damage.

The nutritionist emphasized the fact that oral antibiotics can cause changes in the intestinal walls which can bring about a problem with the absorption of nutrients. Notably, if antibiotics are given frequently, bacteria within the body can develop a resistance to the drug, rendering the drug helpless against a truly life-threatening illness. This warning regarding antibiotics is reason enough to guard against the abuse of the drug with children and adults alike.

"All drugs are toxic; all are potential poisons; and it is for this reason that [so many] are sold only on prescription," says Davis. Drugs work by interfering with the natural enzyme system of the body while attacking the pathogen (or problem). What this means is that the drug often causes damage while treating the ailment. In contrast, nutrients work less quickly, but build the enzymatic system rather than interfere with it, assisting the body by making it less vulnerable to pathogens.

One interference that drugs cause is to counteract vitamin absorption. For this reason, Davis highly recommends vitamin supplements when taking drugs. She taught that Vitamin C increase was beneficial during any kind of drug ingestion, for example, and that 10 milligrams of B6 given to a child on antibiotics might prevent complications. For children six months and older she adds that, "If oral antibiotics are used, yogurt or acidophilus milk or culture should always be given daily with the drug and for three weeks or more afterward to replace valuable intestinal bacteria." The problem is that few people are aware of a nutrient absorption problem associated with taking drugs. Even more significant is the fact that few medical doctors have the training to make a nutritional judgment in this arena.

Davis did not discount the value of medicine, but clearly pointed out the value of nutrition and supplementation that medicine is only beginning to acknowledge. For example, with childhood problems such as hyperactivity, MD's prescribe drugs including Ritalin. Davis, on the other hand, recommended dietary changes, in particular, the removal of foods that cause an allergic reaction in the child.[4]

Hundreds of illnesses—temporary, chronic and terminal—proliferate through each generation, and most still exist at the same or increasing levels of severity, without any significant help from medical science. Granted, major improvements in specific technologies including many in emergency medicine and surgery have encouraged both life and quality of life, but much of medicine dealing with chronic ailments and disease is no further along than it was in years past.

The reason for this, according to William Philpott, MD, and Dwight Kalita, Ph.D, is the nature of most modern medicine. In their book, *Brain Allergies, The Psychonutrient Connection,* the doctors refer to the therapy chosen by most physicians during the last fifty years, that therapy being toximolecular or drug therapy, the application of drugs at sublethal levels.

> **Drugs, of course, are alien chemicals which are not normally present in the cellular environment of the human body. They radically alter man's biochemical-physiological internal environment and often occasion very severe and dangerous side effects. Needless to say, drugs do not halt or prevent the disease process, especially degenerative disease; at best they offer symptomatic relief, while the fundamental, underlying disease process continues uninterrupted.**

In the same book, Dr. Roger J. Williams is quoted from his work, *Nutrition Against Disease:*

> The basic fault of these weapons [drugs] is that they have no known connection with the disease process itself...Drugs are wholly unlike nature's weapons...They tend to mask the difficulty, not eliminate it. They contaminate the internal environment [with side effects], create dependence on the part of the patient, and often complicate the physician's job by erasing valuable clues as to the real source of the trouble.

Philpott and Kalita cite several examples to make their point, particularly with the use of drugs in treating mental illness and the use of tranquilizers. Side effects associated with long-term use of these drugs include allergic skin reactions, allergic bone marrow reaction, hepatitis, and deterioration of the heart that can result in death.

Although the association and frequency of side effects is debated by supporters of these drugs, to Philpott and Kalita the evidence is clear:

> Using an injectable phenothiazine tranquilizer in a controlled study on rats, one researcher demonstrated a 20 percent loss of brain cells in the corpus stratum. This experiment shows the significance of a phenothiazine [tranquilizer] producing destructive reaction in the brain area responsible for parkinsonism [deterioration of the nervous system] and tardive dyskinesia. Microscopic evidence proves that this occurs in rats; clinical evidence indicates that it occurs in humans.

The authors note that many doctors have been fooled by the short-term benefits of tranquilizers. Awareness is now growing that with this type of drug the side effects can be as serious as the illness, and that even though the patient is tranquilized, there is still underlying illness. Quality of life continues to deteriorate as long as the patient is maintained on a drug course.

At the end of their discussion of tranquilizers and toximolecular medicine versus a nutrient approach, Philpott and Kalita say that our healthcare system needs doctors who are interested in curing and preventing disease rather than those who are concerned with masking the symptoms. They point to nutrient therapy as an important answer which they say is safe and economical and most importantly, prevention-oriented.[5]

The major killers of the 1990s—heart disease, cancer and diabetes, for example, continue to plague Americans. Medical treatment for each illness has rendered no significant progress in defeating them. Yet, despite the colossal failure of orthodox medical methods, little has been done to mainstream alternative approaches to health that might yield gains.

Dean Black, Ph.D., in his book *Health at the Crossroads*, addresses the barrier to mainstreaming alternative approaches. He writes:

> It's interesting to note that one effect of our current healthcare laws is to block the flow of information.
>
> I can sell just about any health product I want [without FDA approval] as long as I don't tell you what's it's supposed to do, or why I think it will work. To give you that information, I've got to get it approved by the Food and Drug Administration, which approves virtually nothing but medical research.

Dr. Black points out that research on vitamins, herbs and most other nonmedical avenues exists, but that this research has not met FDA requirements. So although alternative treatments and products can be marketed without the FDA's nod of approval, no one can make a claim to the public that they can be used for specific illnesses, i.e. that Vitamin E can help strengthen the heart.

Black emphasizes that in order for claims to be made, someone would have to underwrite the high pricetag of FDA approval—a minimum of $70 million per product—to run the obstacle course the administration requires. Unfortunately, with substances like vitamins, minerals and herbs, a no-win situation exists because even if someone were willing to underwrite the millions in research—for example, to prove that Vitamin E can help lower cholesterol, Vitamin E cannot be patented because it is a naturally occurring substance. So approval would mean that any business interest could use the FDA's approval and market Vitamin E with the specific claim that it helps lower cholesterol, leaving the underwriter $70 million poorer with no edge on the market.

On the other side, pharmaceutical companies realize an edge because drugs are chemical compounds. Once a company has achieved FDA approval on a drug, it will reap several years of profit before competitors are allowed to create their own version of that drug once the original patent has expired.

Black states that:

> The net effect of our current laws is to set up a filter that passes only certain kinds of information about health products and therapies. Studies of drugs pass the filter, studies of herbs and nutrients don't. . . nor does information about [nonmedical] remedies.

To Black, it is only common sense to understand that if these treatments held no value, they would have faded away long ago.[6] Yet the pharmaceutical industry has worked diligently in an effort to diminish alternatives to medical care.

The power pharmaceutical companies enjoy stems from almost a century of political maneuvering, whereby over time, doctors, medical schools, insurance companies and the government became puppets under drug company control. Over time, drug companies were able to convince these vital parties that health care and pharmaceuticals are synonymous, that health care could not exist unless drugs were involved. The other piece to that control existed with the public, convincing them that drugs are good, that drugs are health-enhancing, that there is a pill for every ailment and an ailment for every pill.

The public's approval of drugs is evident in the following combination of statistics from a 1992 *USA Today* showing the total expenditure for drugs in the United States, the population for those selected years and dollars spent on drugs per person:

Year	Money Spent on Drugs		
	$$ Spent (Billions)	US Population	$$ Spent Per Person
1981	$20.7	229,966,000	$90
1983	$24.5	234,307,000	$105
1985	$28.7	238,466,000	$120
1991	$46.6	252,643,000	$184
1992	$56.7	255,407,000	$222
1997*	$103.25	268,702,000	$384
*Projected			

In his book, *Assault on Medical Freedom*, P. Joseph Lisa quotes figures from the U.S. Office of Management and Budget (OMB), noting that it can be projected at current increases, by 1997, Americans will spend $103.25 billion on drugs (or $384 per person, a more than 400% per person increase over 1981, just 16 years earlier.) The author writes, "The term 'big business' does not adequately describe the stake the pharmaceutical manufacturers have in the future of drugs."

Alternative avenues of health care are the direct competition of the medical industry, and products including vitamins, minerals and herbs, are the direct product competition of the pharmaceutical industry since if these alternatives work to help diminish illness or even cure illness by building health, the result is a diminished need for drugs.

In order to prevent this from happening, Lisa describes a campaign that began in 1983 when the Pharmaceutical Advertising Council (PAC) and the United States Food and Drug Administration (FDA) entered a joint campaign which they called a Public Service Anti-Quackery Campaign. Under the guise of public service the coalition's goal was to further discredit "quacks" (the competitors of the drug industry) in the eyes of the government, the media and the public. The campaign was largely funded by pharmaceutical companies and executed in part by Grey Medical Advertising, a New York-based firm that stood as one of the largest medical advertising firms in the world.

Lisa writes:

> The most chilling and bizarre aspect of this unholy alliance between the FDA and the pharmaceutical industry is that the very industry the FDA should be looking into, the drug industry, is instead the FDA's partner in a campaign designed to direct the FDA at the drug industry's economic competitors. Instead of policing the drug industry, the FDA is going after targets the drug industry says need to be investigated and prosecuted. The result of such an anti-competitive alliance is, of course, the destruction of the economic competitors of the pharmaceutical houses.[7]

As long as the FDA and the drug industry are bed partners, critics say that health care expenditures will continue to escalate at alarming rates. As long as there is no true competition for health care dollars, the industry can continue to charge whatever it wants even though no gains are made in our state of national health. If this trend continues and we are spending $384 a year for every man, woman and child in this country in 1997, by the year 2007 we will be trying to find a way to pay for thousands of dollars per person for drugs. If the medical monopoly still exists into the next century—if somehow this country does not come to terms with the truth, that medicine is simply not working, at least in this monopolistic state, we will truly know what it means to have an impoverished nation, a vulnerable nation because of a population too sick to care.

1. "Preventive Medicine for Our Ailing Health Care System," Alexander Leaf, MD, *Journal of the American Medical Association (JAMA)*, February 3, 1993.

2. *Male Practice, How Doctors Manipulate Women*, Robert S. Mendelsohn, MD, Contemporary Books, Inc., Chicago, 1982.

3. Information provided by the Michigan Midwives Association, (1988 Statistics), Route 1, Hesperia, Michigan, 48421,

4. *Let's Have Healthy Children,* Adelle Davis (Revised by Marshall Mandell, MD), Signet, New York, 1981.

5. *Brain Allergies, The Psychonutrient Connection*, William H. Philpott, MD and Dwight K. Kalita, Ph.D., Keats Publishing, Inc., New Canaan, Connecticut 1980.

6. *Health at The Crossroads*, Dean Black, Ph.D., Springdale Press, 1988.

7. *The Assault on Medical Freedom*, P. Josph Lisa, Hampton Roads Publishing Company, Norfolk, VA, Chapters 4 and 8, 1994.

5

Deadly Drugs from The Prescription Pad

In the United States, the Food and Drug Administration (FDA) approves, regulates and monitors all medications and medical devices. Yet, more than twenty years ago, Ralph Nader decided that the FDA wasn't doing its job; it wasn't protecting the public's interest. As a result, "Public Citizen" was founded. Although Public Citizen is not the only public advocacy group looking at pharmaceutical products with a questioning eye, it's one of the most visible.

Public Citizen's five divisions include "Congress Watch," a branch involved with consumer-related legislation on

Capitol Hill. Next, there is "The Litigation Group," which serves as a public interest law firm bringing before the court precedent-setting lawsuits on the public's behalf. There is also "The Critical Mass Energy Project," which calls for a decrease in nuclear and fossil fuels; and the "Buyers Up" division, a home heating oil cooperative which acts as an information bank on home energy and environmental issues. Its fifth division, Health Research Group (HRG), was set up as a watchdog of the FDA, and the pharmaceutical and medical device industry.

For more than two decades, the Health Research Group has reported, petitioned and testified to the press and particularly to the federal government on the safety and efficacy of products used in the health care industry. Many of these products are prescription drugs, some of which are considered unsafe at any dosage.

Over the past twenty years, HRG efforts have played an important role in policing dozens of prescription and over-the-counter drugs linked to side effects posing serious health threats and even the possibility of death for those who take them. Depending on each drug's nature, the division's goal has been to restrict prescriptions, increase labeling warnings and, in many cases, remove a drug from the market if reports of complications during usage prove that its side effects are more dangerous than the benefits it provides.

Why the FDA itself hasn't done a better job policing the drug industry is a good question, one a number of groups similar to HRG have asked. Yet the fact remains, when a publicly-funded government-run operation like the FDA doesn't do its job, the responsibility falls back on the public itself. The public must police the police.

The following list comprises a sampling of drugs HRG has listed as potentially dangerous medications, the side effects each can cause, as well as the year(s) HRG's major efforts took place:

Popular Drugs Listed by HRG as Potentially Dangerous

Drug and Treatment	Complications
Accutane ('80's) severe cystic acne	Birth defects, spontaneous abortions
Alka Seltzer ('73) stomach upset	Gastrointestinal bleeding
Alupent ('83) metered dose inhalers	Asthma deaths
Miscellaneous antibiotics ('84) infections	Misuse and antibiotic resistance
Antivert ('88) vertigo	(Promotion depicted an ironworker working on a high-rise building even though the drug can cause drowsiness.)
Arlidin ('84) vasodilator	Ineffective
Aspirin ('82-'85), miscellaneous	Can be a catalyst in development of Reye's Syndrome in children
Benedictin, ('81-''83) morning sickness	Risk of birth defects
Benzodiazepines ('81-90s) sleeping pills/tranquilizers	Erratic behavior
Estrogens and other hormones ('78-90s) birth control, menopause symptom control	Cancer, heart disease
Bromocriptine ('88) lactation suppression	Unnecessary and can cause blood clots
Buspar ('87) tranquilizer	Promotion depicted use by anxious air traffic controller

Butazolidin/Tandearil ('83) arthritis/anti-inflammatory	Reported deaths
Chloroform ('75), ingredient in medicines	Carcinogenic
Clindamycin/Lincomycin ('75) antibiotic	Overprescribing of this strong antibiotic
Clofibrate ('79-'81) cholesterol lowering	Ineffectiveness and increased mortality rate
Clozapine ('91) antipsychotic	Respiratory arrest risk even after first dose particularly in patients taking benzodiazepines such as Valium, Halcion and Xanax; and fatal blood disease
Cyclospasmol ('84) vasodilators or circulation enhancer	Not proven effective for any condition
Dalmane ('83) sedative/tranquilizer	Dangerous side effects including dizziness, impairment of mental facilities, memory loss and addiction especially in 60+ age group (typical of most benzodiazepine drugs)
Darvon ('78-80) narcotic/pain relief	Darvon-related deaths often by overdose (proven to be no more effective than aspirin)
Depo-Provera ('75-'90s) progestin used for birth control/hormone for menopause symptoms	Risk of cancer and bone density decrease, possibility of blood clot, stroke, blindness
Diethylstilbestrol ('72-'85)	Cancer in users, and

miscarriage prevention

their offspring

Diabetes drugs ('77)
anti-diabetes

Unsafe, ineffective and
over-prescribed

Febrile seizure drugs ('80)
febrile convulsions

Misuse

Feldene ('86)
anti-arthritic

Life-threatening,
gastro-intestinal
bleeding particularly
in older patients

Fentanyl ('89)
narcotic lollipops for children

Misuse

Flagyl ('74)
anti-bacterial

Shown to cause
cancer, gene
mutations and birth
defects in animal tests

Guaifenesin ('83)
expectorant, cold drug

Not proven effective

Halcion ('90's)
tranquilizer

Erratic behavior,
impairment of mental
abilities

Hydergine ('91),
Alzheimer's

Alzheimer's
disease

Ineffective and
possibly harmful, i.e.
might accelerate

Ilosone ('79)
antibiotic

Liver damage

Librium ('84)
tranquilizer
(also see Dalmane,
Halcion)

Promotions that are
false and misleading

Nizoral ('83)
fungus infections

Liver damage and
death

Oraflex ('82)*
anti-arthritic

Liver and kidney
damage, death

Paroxitine ('91)** anti-depressant	Promoting drug when it had not been deemed safe or effective by FDA
Phenergan ('88) anti-nausea, antihis-tamine, antipsychotic	Sudden Infant Death connections (SIDS); drug-induced parkinsonism and involuntary movement lasting an indefinite period of time, mental impairment.
Phenformin ('77) anti-diabetes	Imminent hazard
Phenylpropanolamine ('83) anti-obesity	Lack of safety and efficacy
Prozac ('91) antidepressant	Erratic behavior or suicidal thoughts
Quinine Sulfate ('88) leg cramps	Fatal bleeding disorders, generally unsafe and ineffective
Relafon ('91)** anti-inflammatory	Promoting drug when it had not been deemed safe or effective by the FDA
Selacryn* ('80's) antihypertensive	Drug manufacturer failed to report injuries in patients using Selacryn
Suprol ('86) for arthritis	Acute renal failure and pain
Valium ('80) tranquilizers, sleeping aid	(See Dalmane, Halcion)
Versed ('88) sedative	Injury and death

The following two cases exemplify FDA actions taken as a result of HRG's actions:

> *Eli Lilly and Company (Oraflex) and the SmithKline Corporation (Selacryn) received criminal prosecution for failing to report adverse reactions experienced with these drugs to the FDA.

> **Public Citizen Health Research group petitioned the FDA in 1991 urging them to criminally prosecute SmithKline Beecham for violating federal drug laws when the company promoted Relafon and Paroxitine; neither had been deemed safe and effective by the FDA. [1]

Many of the drugs Health Research Group labeled "Do Not Use" or "Limited Use" in their publication *Worst Pills Best Pills II* [2], continue to appear on the top-selling product list. It doesn't appear the warning is being acknowledged by those who should listen most intently to such messages: the doctors prescribing the drugs. What follows is a list of best selling drugs during the years 1992 through 1995 as well as comments including side effects listed in *Worst Pills Best Pills*.

Drugs Dispensed Most Often in U.S. Community Pharmacies: [3]

(Total Prescriptions, All Strengths)

1992		1993		1994	
1.	Premarin	1.	Premarin	1.	Premarin
2.	Amoxil	2.	Zantac	2.	Zantac
3.	Zantac	3.	Amoxil	3.	Amoxil
4.	Lanoxin	4.	Synthroid	4.	Synthroid
5.	Synthroid	5.	Procardia	5.	Lanoxin
6.	Procardia	6.	Lanoxin	6.	Procardia
7.	Xanax	7.	Xanax	7.	Vasotec
8.	Vasotec	8.	Trimox	8.	Trimox
9.	Cardizem	9.	Vasotec	9.	Cardizem
10.	Ceclor	10.	Cardizem	10.	Prozac

Drugs Dispensed Most Often in U.S.
Community Pharmacies, 1995

(Total Prescriptions, New and Refill)

1.   Premarin Tabs
2.   Trimox
3.   Synthroid
4.   Amoxil
5.   Zantac
6.   Lanoxin
7.   Procardia XL
8.   Vasotec
9.   Prozac
10.   Proventil Aerosol

(*American Druggist* altered its classification of "The Top 200 Drugs" in 1995 to "Total Prescriptions, New and Refill." In earlier years, including those listed here from 1992-94, the "Top 200" classification read, "Total Prescriptions, All Strengths." This re-classification amounts to a re-positioning of most drugs listed in the top ten best selling drugs. *Still nine out of ten remain in the top ten in 1995 from the year before.* To avoid confusion due to this re-classification, 1995 rankings will not be discussed below.)

The number one drug, Premarin (Wyeth-Ayerst), is a drug suggested for "Limited Use" by HRG. Yet, in spite of its potential risk, Premarin has reigned as the top-selling pharmaceutical product for 1992, 1993 and 1994. Prescribed as estrogen-replacement therapy for post-menopausal women, Premarin has been linked by studies to serious side effects, including a 30 percent increased risk of breast cancer in women who use the drug for 15 years and a 50 percent increased risk in breast cancer for women who take menopausal estrogen for 25 years.

Scientific studies are rated by the quality of the research. The testing elements in studies labeled "highest quality" are considered the most accurate of all studies evaluated. When pharmaceutical studies considered of lesser accuracy are removed from consideration, the outlook is even more grim. Standing alone, the "high quality" tests showed that women who take menopausal estrogen for 15 years risk not a 30 percent increase, but a *60 percent* increase in breast cancer while those women taking the drug for 25 years, risked, not a 50 percent increased risk, but a *100 percent* increased risk, or a doubling in their personal risk of cancer.[4]

Estrogen is also linked to other types of cancers. (See Chapter 7, "Women—The Captive Market.)" Estrogen has also been found to cause vaginal discharge and bleeding, drowsiness, urination problems, headache, loss of coordination, pain, shortness of breath, slurred speech, vision abnormalities and weakness or numbness in the arms and legs, high blood pressure, uncontrolled movement of the body, breast lumps or discharge, mental depression, stomach or side pain, yellowing of the eyes or skin, skin rash, bloating, cramping, nausea, loss of appetite, weight change, breast swelling or tenderness, changes in sexual appetite, changes in hair growth, diarrhea, dizziness irritability, decreased tolerance to wearing contact lenses.

Zantac (Glaxo) ranked as the #2 best selling drug in both 1993 and 1994, and #3 in 1992. Usually prescribed for ulcers and other conditions related to excess stomach acid, drugs in this category can cause confusion as well as reduced kidney and liver function, particularly in older patients. Other side effects reported include hallucinations, sore throat and fever, unusual bleeding or bruising, irregular heartbeat, tiredness or weakness, as well as constipation, diarrhea, dizziness, headache, nausea, skin rash, and stomach pain.

The antibiotic Amoxil held the #3 position in both 1993 and 1994, and the #2 position in 1992. Produced by at least three pharmaceutical companies, the drug can create side effects including pain, cramping, bloating, diarrhea that may contain blood; fever, nausea, thirst, weakness or tiredness, weight loss, skin rash, yellowing of eyes or skin and appetite loss. Concern about antibiotic overload can also be considered a side effect.

Synthroid, a thyroid-replacement hormone, ranked #4 in 1993 and 1994, and #5 in 1992. *Worst Pills Best Pills* reports that it is unnecessarily prescribed for most people taking it, in particular for those whose thyroid levels are well in the normal range. Complications include chest pain, rapid or irregular heartbeat, change in appetite, vomiting, weight loss or gain, constipation, diarrhea, fever, tremors, headache, irritability, muscle aches, cramping, nervousness, heat/cold sensitivity, shortness of breath, sleeping problems, skin problems, coordination loss and fatigue.

Lanoxin, #5 in 1994, #6 in 1993, and #4 in 1992, is prescribed to treat symptoms of heart failure including arrhythmia. The drug can be highly toxic. One in five people taking the drug develops drug toxicity. Ironically in spite of this side effect, the drug is overprescribed and four out of ten people taking it realize no benefits from what is generically called digitalis. *Worst Pills* warns also of a significant interaction with a long list of other drugs.

Of the five remaining drugs included in the top ten best selling drugs, the risks are also disturbing. The #6 best selling drug in 1994 and #5 best selling drug in 1993 was Procardia, a calcium channel blocker, used for hypertension, chest pain and coronary artery disease.

HRG reports that each calcium channel blocker varies in the possibility of causing harmful side effects—the bad news. HRG's good news: that these blockers appear to improve a patient's capacity for exercise, leading to a possible delay in the need for heart surgery.

However, what HRG has not mentioned in their reference book is a more serious complication possibility, that the six million Americans now taking calcium channel blockers are possibly increasing their risk of heart attack by 60 percent. These findings were reported by Bruce Psaty, an epidemiologist at the University of Washington in Seattle, in a research study which hit the Associated Press wire service in March of 1995. Psaty believes those at risk also include relatively healthy people who are using the channel blockers purely as a preventive measure.[5]

The University of Washington study drew heated criticism from medical professionals throughout the country, who countered by saying the study was not conclusive. However, other members of the medical community agreed that the possibility of heart attack risk may exist.

Health Research Group says that changes in lifestyle including diet (less salt and alcohol), losing weight, and exercising more serve as the best way to lower high blood pressure. When that doesn't work, they clearly recommend medication such as channel blockers, yet HRG doesn't mention that there is significant controversy regarding the basic efficacy of this medication. Critics including Dr. Psaty consider calcium channel blockers an ineffective tool against hypertension. If the effectiveness is not apparent, they say, why risk the side effects?

Previous studies have also demonstrated that calcium channel blockers can prove dangerous when given to help prevent another heart attack from occurring.

Studies pointing both to the dangers of heart attack caused by channel blockers and the drug's overall inefficacy date back several years, yet *Worst Pills Best Pills* II edition does not mention these allegations. The book does refer to a number of possible side effects, the most serious being chest pain, dizziness, headache, discoloration, swelling, drowsiness, weakness and irregular heartbeat. Perhaps the mention of "chest pain" is a loose reference to possible heart attack, but if so, it is unclear.

Paul Ridker, M.D., a cardiologist and epidemiologist at the Brigham and Women's Hospital in Boston, was mentioned in the Associated Press story that focused on Psaty's work. Dr. Ridker says that medical doctors continue prescribing calcium channel blockers despite the evidence of inefficacy and health risk primarily because the pharmaceutical companies have pushed the drug so well.

In fact, the top ten list of best selling drugs reads like a Who's Who from year to year, the stars making the list over and over again. The only real difference between 1993 and 1994, for example, was the elimination of Upjohn's tranquilizer Xanax. Holding the position of #7 in both 1992 and 1993, it dropped to position #28 in 1994 once its patent protection ran out and generic competition heated up.

Xanax itself is labeled, "Do Not Use" by HRG as it is in the category known as Benzodiazepines (sleeping pills and tranquilizers), the same drug family as Halcion, Valium, Ativan, Librium, Tranxene, Prosom, Dalmane, Paxipam, Centrax, Doral and Restoril. Of a long list of side effects, the most serious include mental impairment, memory loss, dizziness, increased risk of accidents and addiction.

Depending on their composition, the effects of drugs can frequently be unpredictable. For example, some benzodiazepines stay in the body for such a long duration that a person might still be sedated the next day, while other benzodiazepines are short-lasting, leaving a patient vulnerable to rebound insomnia and associated confusion. Drugs in this category have thus been demonstrated as initiating the same condition they are supposed to remedy: insomnia.

Now in Xanax's former spot, Vasotec rose to the #7 position in 1994, from #9 the previous year. Vasotec is prescribed as a high blood pressure (antihypertensive) medication. Serious side effects include the most significant ones: causing bone marrow depression and kidney disease.

The #8 position for both 1993 and 1994 was held by Trimox, a drug in the antibiotic/penicillin family. Although often prescribed for a spectrum of illness, these drugs can cause serious side effects including anaphylactic shock, which can be fatal, and other severe reactions including asthma, weakness, pain, nausea, diarrhea, rash and toxicity.

Labeled "Limited Use" in *Worst Pills*, #9 in 1992 and 1994 and #10 in 1993, Cardizem is another calcium channel blocker in the same family as Procardia. Channel blockers have been associated with a 60 percent increased risk of heart attack, according to the University of Washington study referenced earlier. In general, antihypertensives open the user to a number of possible side effects without adequate proof of the drug's therapeutic value.

As mentioned, some studies have also demonstrated that calcium channel blockers are dangerous when given to people who have recently had heart attacks, as well as when given to people to prevent a second one.

Prozac completes the top-selling list for 1994 at #10. The controversy over this particular anti-depressant is well-documented, particularly as a cause of suicidal tendencies. However, doctors continue to prescribe Prozac at the same frequency as before, showing with their prescription pads their strong support for the drug. Critics have wondered if the rash of pro-Prozac literature (including several books) might be a well-orchestrated promotional tactic initiated by Prozac's manufacturer to boost sales in spite of the risks.

In light of Prozac's reported dangers, Health Research Group (the Ralph Nader organization) provides a warning, although lukewarm, regarding the drug:

> A small number of people taking [Prozac] have experienced intense, violent, suicidal thoughts, agitation, and impulsivity. Whether their symptoms were induced by [Prozac] or were related to their underlying psychological problems is unclear. As with any other antidepressant, [Prozac] should only be used under close medical supervision.

Beyond the possibility of these side effects, other complications can include nausea, anxiety, headache and insomnia, while most adverse effects are thought to be experienced primarily during the first days of taking the drug. Other effects can include restlessness, constant pacing, purposeless movements, dry mouth, sweating, diarrhea, tremor, loss of appetite and dizziness.

Finally, all of the drugs mentioned in the top-selling list have been found to cause significant and often dangerous interactions when taken with certain other drugs.

For example, the estrogen Premarin is known to react with some cortisone-based drugs; barbiturates (a class of drugs intended primarily for use as anticonvulsants, but often misused as painkillers); some antibiotics; Bromocriptine (an antiparkinsonian drug) and others. It should be emphasized that this is Premarin, the best-selling drug in the United States.

Yet, these potentially dangerous drugs are highly promoted. The estrogen Premarin, manufactured by Wyeth-Ayerst, is a prime example. Of the 1992 share of ad dollars, in percentages, Premarin's advertising grabbed second place, with 1.75 percent of advertising dollars spent for all pharmaceutical products and services in the U.S. that year.

The most-advertised drug in 1992 was Neupogen, manufactured by Amgen Biolog, which made up 2.09 percent of all dollars spent for pharmaceutical product and services advertising in the U.S. that year. Neupogen is marketed primarily to offset side effects of chemotherapy. A primary application of Neupogen is to ward off infection that might set in since chemotherapy often weakens the immune system. Yet, a note of warning in the *Physicians' Desk Reference* (1995) reads:

> **Neupogen is a growth factor that primarily stimulates neutrophils [having to do with blood cells]. However, the possibility that Neupogen can act as a growth factor for any tumor type, particularly myeloid malignancies, cannot be excluded. Therefore, because of the possibility of tumor growth, precaution should be exercised in using this drug in any malignancy with myeloid characteristics.**

Conclusion: Neupogen is a drug used to potentially offset the effects of another drug, namely chemotherapy, but its use can possibly cause additional cancer growth.

In descending order, the following side effects have also been experienced in patients during Neupogen drug trials: nausea/vomiting, skeletal pain, alopecia [baldness], diarrhea, fever and others.[6]

Critics of the drug industry insist that heavy promotion by drug manufacturers amounts to patient exploitation. Drug promotion offers doctors and patients hope, but too often that hope is false. The drug may hold the potential of causing more harm than good, and even create side effects that require yet another drug.

Other drugs on the top ten list for sales were also in the top ten most advertised products during 1992. Cardizem CD, (Marion Merrell-Dow), was in #5 position in advertising expenditures with 1.30 percent of all advertising dollars. The cholesterol-lowering drug Pravachol (B-M Squibb), an unranked drug for sales success in 1992, attained the position of #105 in 1993, and then moved up to #75 in 1994. Advertising expenditures for Pravachol in 1992 ranked it as the #6 most advertised pharmaceutical with 1.23 percent of advertising dollars spent that year. As the #4 most advertised pharmaceutical in 1992, Verelan (Lederle) grabbed 1.48 percent of advertising dollars, moving it from position #140 in 1992 to #128 in 1993, and #127 in 1994.[7]

Pharmaceutical advertising comes with another price, one ultimately paid for in increased prices by the consumer. Once a drug is highly prescribed by doctors and their patients rely on it, manufacturers can use product loyalty and popularity to bolster profits by raising prices. Between 1985 and 1991 the following drugs increased dramatically in price:[8]

1. *Premarin* 148 percent increase (estrogen)

2. Inderal 129 percent increase (anti-hypertensive)

3. Lopressor 118 percent increase (anti-hypertensive)

4. *Synthroid* 110 percent increase (thyroid hormone replacement)

5. *Xanax* 106 percent increase (tranquilizer)

6. Feldene 92 percent increase (anti-inflammatory)

7. *Procardia* 90 percent increase (anti-hypertensive)

8. Capoten 85 percent increase (anti-hypertensive)

9. *Ceclor* 82 percent increase (antibiotic)

10. *Zantac* 66 percent increase (stomach acid blocker)

(Brand names in italics are for drugs listed in the top ten best-selling pharmaceutical products in one or more years from 1992 to 1994.)

With over 2,800 drugs now listed in the 1995 *Physicians' Desk Reference*, pharmaceutical companies say that in order to make their products known, they need to promote as they do. They have this right in a free market system as well as the right to charge what they believe is necessary.

Alarmed observers disagree, stating that *all* promotion of drugs should be regulated, not just the somewhat-regulated practice of offering direct gifts and other incentives to doctors. Other areas of promotion and advertising the FDA should equally scrutinize include pharmaceutical marketing directed to pharmacists, nurses, hospital administrators and to patients as well as doctors. Manufacturer-sponsored seminars labeled "educational" when the actual motive is drug promotion should also be regulated.

According to Scott-Levin Associates, a pharmaceutical marketing service in Newton, Pennsylvania, drug promotion has played an increasingly significant role in prescribing trends. For example, in 1987, just 18 percent of patients asked doctors about specific drugs. In 1992, following a major upswing in pharmaceutical advertising directed to the consumer, 54 percent of patients were asking their doctors about specific drugs,[9] demonstrating the effectiveness of directing advertising to a public virtually ignorant of the undesirable effects drugs might have. This represents a serious ethical concern.

Scott-Levin also pointed out that a 40 percent increase in the number of pharmaceutical sales representatives between 1980 and 1990 started a fire in prescribing trends that fueled pharmaceutical profits. A typical doctor will see roughly two drug company reps each week. According to *Fortune* magazine's Value Line Institutional Services, the industry's return on sales had been steady at around 10 percent (profit as the percentage of the industry's total sales revenue). From 1980 on, however, profit as a percent of sales began rising dramatically while in other major industries—including computers and office equipment, motor vehicles and parts, food, petroleum and publishing/printing—the profit-sales ratio remained relatively constant.

Pharmaceutical companies are the most profitable industry in the U.S., whether that profit is measured by return on equity, return on assets or as a percent of sales.[10]

Drugs become best sellers in the same way that Coca Cola and McDonald's achieve market shares. A lot of marketing done well, works. There is, however, a significant difference. While consumers generally realize that Coke and Big Mac's are not the most nutritious foods to eat, these foods don't come with long lists of side effects that can be dangerous or even fatal at any size of serving. And while the commercials pushing Coca Cola and Big Macs may be hyped or even misleading, lunch is not the same as a drug. Drugs should not be promoted like fast food as if these chemicals were the best thing that ever happened to mankind. Drugs and Big Macs cannot be promoted with equal indiscretion.

We don't like to think that our doctor is probably prescribing a drug for us that has been thrust in front of him (or in front of us) more than any other in its class through highly effective promotional strategies. Most of us would like to think that our doctors aren't as vulnerable to pharmaceutical marketing strategies as the public is to fast food commercials. Truth is, they are.

The predictable response by the pharmaceutical company is that only a small number of those taking a drug experience any kind of serious problems. The same could be said about living near a landfill, working in a chemical company, or smoking cigarettes. The more you are exposed to risk, the greater your potential of harm. Eli Lilly's remark about drugs may be appropriate here. The drug magnate said that a drug without toxic effects is not a drug at all.

The traditional medical community and its critics usually agree on one point— short-term use of medications is the best way to minimize the risk of side effects. Yet, how many patients are on drugs for the short-term only? Certainly not women who are taking estrogen 15 to 25 years or more, certainly not people supposedly controlling their blood pressure with calcium channel blockers, and certainly not those on heart medications. As is the nature of drugs, few offer any cure, only a supposed modicum of control of an undesirable symptom such as high blood pressure. Patients using many potentially harmful drugs are usually on these medications, with all their side effects, for life.

Does "short term" cover popping an ibuprofen or acetaminophen tablet for that frequent run-of-the-mill headache? Medical reports during the past few years have led to wholesale recommendations that people should take one aspirin every day in order to help prevent heart attack. Later, follow-up studies warned that regular aspirin use might cause serious health problems including ulcers with regular, long-term use. Yet, that first report encouraged people to take an aspirin a day, and many still are.

Realistically, then, is short-term use of a drug possible when pharmaceutical companies are only satisfied with the public's long-term, regular usage, since profits multiply with regular pill usage compared with occasional use? A steady audience is clearly a more lucrative one.

Pharmaceutical companies have done a brilliant job marketing their products, but in doing so, they have demonstrated a critical lack of prudence in the high-level promotion of potentially dangerous drugs. At best, the industry provides an excellent model of how marketing earns profits while good marketing earns more of it. At worst, the industry shows that its concern for profits outweighs a concern for ethics and public welfare.

Perhaps the drug industry deserves signs of their own that could be posted on the storefronts of every pharmacy and on the front landscapes of every pharmaceutical company in America. These signs could read, "Billions Served. Billions More Made!" Sadly enough, these are the tangible signs of a free market system that has gone too far. One might hardly notice the small letters at the sign's base reading, "Proceed at your own risk."

1. Public Citizen documents describing action Health Research Group (HRG) has taken on individual pharmaceutical products. Health Research Group, 2000 P Street, NW, Washington, DC 20036.

2. *Worst Pills Best Pills II*, Public Citizen's Health Research Group, Washington, D.C., 1993.

3. "Drugs Dispensed Most Often in U.S. Community Pharmacies," *American Druggist,* February 1994, Pg. 28; February 1995, Pg 21; and February 1996, pg. 19.

4. "A Meta-Analysis of the Effect of Estrogen Replacement Therapy on the Risk of Breast Cancer," Steinberg, Thacker, Smith et al, (Centers for Disease Control Study), *Journal of the American Medical Association (JAMA),* Sept. 11, 1991.

5. "Blood Pressure drugs may increase heart attack risk," Paul Raeburn, The Associated Press, March 10, 1995.

6. *Physician's Desk Reference*, 1995.

7. "Most advertised pharmaceutical products/services 1993," *Medical Marketing & Media, Healthcare Advertising Review* (annual), April, 1994, p. 60.

8. "Prescription drugs with the highest price increases (1985-1991)," *Working Woman,* November, 1993, p. 89.

9. *Making Medicine Making Money,* Donald Drake and Marian Uhlman, Andrews and McMeel, pg 26, Kansas City, Missouri, 1993.

10. *Making Medicine Making Money*, pp 6-7, 25, 30.

6

When Doctors Fail

Any drug without toxic effects is not a drug at all.—Eli Lilly

In his book, *Health and Healing,* Andrew Weil, MD, points out that the word "pharmacology" comes from an ancient Greek word meaning poison. He says that in varying dosages, all drugs become poisons even though many poisons are therapeutic in low dosages. Because of this principle of drug usage, toxicity or poisoning is the primary drawback of using prescription drugs. "Adverse drug reactions account for the lion's share of iatrogenic [medically induced] illness— so common that any dedicated patient is sure to experience one sooner or later," Weil writes.

Toxicity is a given for virtually every drug available on the market today even though in order to meet approval standards, drug manufacturers, ironically, must prove the safety of a product. "Safety" is a relative term—relative to

the recommended drug and/or dosage. When it
comes to "safety" in pharmaceutical products,
"safe" does not mean "harmless."

Weil uses two drugs to illustrate this point. Aspirin is
generally considered toxic at ten times the dosage needed to
calm the pain of a bad headache. At this heightened dosage,
salicylate poisoning—a severe reaction—can occur. In stronger drugs such as digitalis (a drug to regulate heartbeat), a
dosage two times the recommended amount can create pre-
cisely the problem the drug is supposed to help, an irregular
heartbeat.[1]

Many drugs can be tragically toxic in any dosage. In the
early 1960's, there was thalidomide, a drug prescribed as a
sedative and hypnotic and most notably used by pregnant
women who subsequently gave birth to children with severe
abnormalities. Fortunately, thalidomide use in the United
States was limited to random testing and not mass distribu-
tion. According to Alan Scott Levin, MD, its tragic side effects gave the FDA good reason to increase federal drug regulation. Before thalidomide, the FDA examined a drug's toxicity; after thalidomide, the agency looked at the side effects of
the drug as well.

The FDA appeared to have the best interest of the public at heart in this move, but what followed gave rise to the
massive growth in profitability for drug manufacturers.
With an added burden of proof, pharmaceutical companies
were required to invest more money in research and development to prove a drug's possible effects. The support of
doctors became more crucial. Doctors would have to be
counted on to prescribe even more in order for the drug to
produce enough revenue to pay off the cost of development
and then make a profit.

Fortunately for the pharmaceutical companies, more
federal dollars became available for healthcare programs.
With the public's increasing concern over their own health,
drug industry profits began to rise. The escalation of marketing efforts directed first to doctors and then to the general public contributed to this growing success.

Much of the advertising associated with pharmaceutical products surrounded claims of "medical breakthroughs,"
whether the claims were actual or invented.

"Detail men" became the major route of reaching the pharmaceutical target market—primarily the M.D. These salespeople, who usually have no formal background in either pharmacology or medicine, became ever more instrumental as the primary avenue for disseminating drug information to doctors. Their job: to visit doctors and distribute information and samples regarding their employer's pharmaceutical products.

Historically, detail representatives have been instructed to entice doctors to prescribe or try their company's drugs by offering them any number of incentives. Gifts, money and even vacations have been freely provided to encourage a doctor to look more closely at a particular company's product. Like any other effective salesperson, the detail rep would quickly point out the negative characteristics of a competitor's products, while pointing out only the positive aspects of his or her own sample bag.[2]

Today, research shows that what doctors know about drugs comes not from their study in formal medical school training, but from the efforts of pharmaceutical companies. These expert marketers push their products through detail salespeople, by sponsoring so-called "continuing education" programs and with promotional literature. John Pekkanen, author of *The American Connection*, agrees. In his book, Pekkanen says, "Contrary to their accepted image and contrary to what the public rightly expects, doctors often know very little about the drugs they are prescribing." This can ultimately lead to mis-diagnosis and error in prescribing drugs.[3]

Drug prescription errors along with other medical mistakes frequently result in serious health problems and can cause iatrogenic or medically caused disease. *The New England Journal of Medicine* published results of the Harvard Medical Practice Study II in which a sample of 30,195 randomly selected hospital records were studied. Of these patients, 3.7 percent were found to have experienced disabling injury due to medical treatment. Complications due to prescribed drugs were the most frequently found adverse reaction at 19 percent; infections followed at 14 percent, while technical complications came in at 13 percent. Of problems reported, approximately 50 percent of negative reactions were related to surgery. The highest proportion of negative reaction was due to diagnostic mishaps.[4]

In his book *Health at the Crossroads,* Dean Black, Ph.D. notes that iatrogenic disease falls into two categories: preventable and non-preventable. Preventable diseases result from mistaken diagnoses, drug and surgical errors that could have been avoided. Non-preventable diseases involve side effects or what doctors consider as necessary health risks to the patient. He notes that the *New England Journal* also reported that 36 percent of 815 consecutive university hospital patients in one study experienced iatrogenic illness and in 2 percent of the 815 patients, the iatrogenic effect was believed to have contributed to patient death.

Black estimates that between 0.5 percent and 2 percent of deaths are death due to iatrogenic illness in U.S. hospitals and that between 1 and 4 million people died between 1981 and 1987 from physician-caused complications.

Black cites the two major theories upon which medicine is built and then points to the error of each. The first principle is the germ theory, that germs cause illness. As an example, he uses the belief that virus causes flu. He says that while it's true that flu cannot be present without virus, it is also true that not everyone exposed to the virus gets the flu. He says the reason for this is that people vary in their adaptive powers, some being more resistant to illness or disease than others. Unfortunately, he points out, medicine doesn't ask how to strengthen the body to avoid disease. What medical practitioners want to know is how to kill the virus. When the germ causing the virus is attacked, the result is that the germ is strengthened, rendering the body's adaptive powers less capable of fighting off the disease.

The same concept can be applied to bacteria. When antibiotics are introduced to the body, the bacteria becomes stronger, rendering the antibiotic less powerful.[5]

Antibiotics can be dangerous. Yet, in various forms they continue to be one of the most widely prescribed drug categories today. Antibiotics are prescribed as a kind of "catch all," for illnesses that include those viral in nature (against which antibiotics are ineffective) and bacterial conditions (against which antibiotics can have an effect). Even so, doctors often show little discretion when weighing the possibility of side effects.

Louise Lander in her book, *Defective Medicine*, notes the downside to prescribing antibiotics. In preventing infection, antibiotics can destroy harmless bacteria that might be helpful in maintaining the delicate balance of the body's internal ecology. These bacteria might also be helpful in keeping other bacteria or fungi in balance. When this balance is thrown off, a "superinfection" can result.[6]

Besides the germ theory, the second and related medical theory, according to Dean Black, is the one of chemical imbalance, that the body can become ill because the chemistry is off. (The body is producing too much or too little of a particular chemical.) Medicine attempts to balance body chemistry by introducing drugs which mimic body chemicals or by introducing drugs that block body chemicals. For example, insulin is introduced to mimic the body's own insulin; antihistamines are introduced to block body histamines. Yet the effect is not as perfect as it might first sound because when the body is exposed to drugs it does an interesting thing—it fights them.

A few examples: When the drug insulin is introduced, it sends a message to the body that the body's own insulin production is adequate; the body slows its own natural insulin production. When the body produces histamines as a reaction to fight allergens, an anti-histamine is often introduced to counter the histamines. If the allergen continues to be present, the body tells itself to make even more histamines, creating a worsened situation than the patient originally experienced. The dosage is then increased or a new drug added to fight the body's reaction. The cycle is a vicious one, Black states. Drug introduction does nothing to strengthen the body's own immune powers or enhance the body's own strength. Instead, medicine tries to replace the healing powers of the body rather than assist them.

Cancer treatment offers another good example. Robert T. Schimke, a noted cancer researcher, points out that che-

motherapy worsens cancer because cancer cells fight the chemotherapy, and this resistance "mimics" the process of cancer.

Black judges medical intervention in this way: "You
can't heal the body by intervening and controlling; you've
got to leave its inner processes alone. Let them do whatever they will at their own imperceptible scale...From this
sort of thinking, natural healing tends to produce neither
side effects nor treatment-caused illnesses." Black implies
that natural healing involves using alternative treatments
that don't cause the body to resist, but support the body as
it uses its own innate healing abilities.

The problem with alternative healing, he asserts, is one
of perception. "The very gentleness that pleases patients
and tends to avoid side effects also produces a certain con-
ceptual and practical fuzziness that makes proving that
natural healing did it almost impossible, at least to the satisfaction of classically trained scientists." Because of this,
established medicine and established science call natural
healing "unscientific." Black disagrees saying it is just a
different way of looking at the body, with its own "methods
of proof."[7]

Medicine considers alternative treatment "non-medicine,"
because it is a contrasting form of health care. Alternative
health care is considered the competition—the enemy, according to practitioners including Dr. Arno Burnier, a Pennsylvania chiropractor, who responded to a March 1993 *Wall
Street Journal* article that crucified the chiropractic profession. Burnier believes the attack was medically initiated as it
came at the height of the Clinton Administration's work in
health care reform. Burnier asserted that the timely attack
in the *Journal* and in other national publications was more
than coincidental and was part of a campaign intended to
sway health care policy makers away from considering chiropractors as primary providers. The attack on chiropractors is
used as an example and is similar to attacks on other nonmedical practitioners.

In a rebuttal to the WSJ article which charged chiropractors with "targeting children simply to expand their
practices and revenue," and as "...fundamentally a nine-
teenth-century philosophy wearing the white smock of sci-

ence," Burnier makes charges of his own, many of which involved medicine's own marketing efforts and often negative results.

Pharmaceutical manufacturers promoted their own products to the American public at a promotional cost of $28 billion dollars in 1992, an alarming fact since adverse drug effects now rank as one of the top causes of hospitalizations and account for as many as 50 million hospital patient days a year. Burnier says, "It is just now being recognized how the assault of these drugs affects immune response and long-range health.

Iatrogenic disease [illness and disease created by medical intervention] affects 20 percent of Americans.

3.5 million surgeries are performed unnecessarily each year resulting in at least 12,000 deaths.

Every 24 to 36 hours, between 50 to 80 percent of all adult Americans consume prescribed medication and each day take at least 52 million aspirin tablets and 30 million sleeping pills.

Burnier says, "Most chiropractors, wellness experts and children's advocates—and even a growing number of medical doctors—regard this as a systematic assault on the internal ecology of the human body." He adds:

The routine use of drugs and antibiotics, along with the ritual of vaccination, is mostly unscientific and based on false assumptions. There is mounting evidence that vaccination programs were introduced when the diseases were already on the decline. The decrease in infectious diseases has now been attributed mainly to improved hygiene, sanitation, nutrition, housing and the natural cycle of those diseases.

Tying the medical issue together, Burnier observes that modern medicine is a practice that arose from Newtonian physics, now centuries old. The problem with this approach is that medicine looks at the body as parts rather than a whole, that "Parts can be taken out or medication can be added to cure [the body]." Burnier charges medicine with arrogance, considering itself the only and final authority on health with the support of law to ensure that its principles and interests are upheld.[8]

Critics of traditional medical practice, including Dr. Robert Mendelsohn, point to a number of medical mistakes during recent years, including medical applications that in the past were accepted as scientifically correct. A sampling of some of the mistakes receiving wide attention are shown in the following table.[9]

Well-Known Pharmaceutical and Medical Mistakes

Treatment/Procedure	Result
X-ray (head, neck, upper chest)	Tens of thousands of thyroid lesions and cancer years later
Diethylstilbestrol (DES) to prevent miscarriage	Tumors/cancer/malformations in offspring's reproductive organs
Aspirin	Stomach lining bleeding, known to cause hemorrhage under the scalp of a newborn if the mother takes this within 72 hours of delivery
Coronary bypass surgery	Often ineffective and deadly
Antihypertensives (blood pressure medication)	Include nausea, loss of sex drive and potency, weakness, (dizziness, muscle cramps, and more)
Antibiotics	Side effects including the possibility of anaphylactic shock, overuse creating a weakening of the body's ability to fight infection, development of superinfections as bacteria develops resistance to each antibiotic
Hyperactive drugs	Growth suppression, high blood pressure, nervousness, insomnia, and creation of zombie-like state

The "dangerous" element in pharmaceuticals involves more than the type of drug. It also involves the administration of the drug—whether the patient is taking the drug unsupervised after a prescription has been written, or whether administration is supervised, for example, given during a hospital stay.

"In 1989, the Joint Commission on Accreditation of Healthcare Organizations reported that the most common problem it found—affecting 88 percent of its hospitals—was failure to evaluate drug usage properly, which is partly the [hospital] pharmacy's responsibility," according to Walt Bogdanich in his book, *The Great White Lie.* Bogdanich states that the accrediting agency rarely revokes accreditation even for serious violations, often letting reports of untrained or poorly trained pharmacy technicians go without investigation or repercussion.[10]

In the book *Medication Errors: Causes and Prevention,* authors N. M. Davis and M.R. Cohen cite the average error rate of hospital-stay drug administration at 12 percent. Applying this to a hospital with 300 patients multiplied by 365 days per year, and an average of ten doses of medication daily per patient, Davis and Cohen estimate that at one hospital more than 131,000 medication errors are committed annually, approximately 360 errors each day.[11]

It is suggested that in order to reduce the incidence of error, prescription drugs should be kept to a minimum, that only those deemed absolutely necessary be prescribed. Yet this plausible solution to the problem, in part, affects the whole of the medical industry: the pharmaceutical company, the doctor, the hospital and all related industries that assist in the production and dispensing of drugs. Every link in the chain would be affected economically, and the political clout of medicine would be reduced. The power of the prescription pad means monetary strength, but is exacted primarily through political might.

Andrew Weil, MD, suggests another way to reduce doctor-induced illness in patients: reduce the use of invasive testing. He believes that the "technological mania that now dominates hospital medicine and medical education makes many people think the older methods of diagnosis are less scientific and therefore less desirable." While he agrees that basic tests including urinalysis, simple x-rays and standard blood tests are important diagnostic tools which usually do not cause much harm, and that high tech testing does have its place, techniques such as the use of dyes and extensive x-raying of the body often cause more harm than good. Harm from inappropriate testing can include death. Weil believes that invasive methods of diagnosing place too much faith in technology and not enough in the doctor.

Weil asserts that diagnosis by technology can also lead to another problem. When a doctor treats the test results rather than the person, abnormalities noted in testing can easily be a result of incorrect diagnosis. For example, in the case of an unclear diagnosis, a patient might be tested until something is found to be wrong and then treated for that condition in order to improve the test result. Or, a patient might be harmed by the tests themselves but receive treatment that conceals those iatrogenic ailments. [12]

In her book, *The Disease Mongers*, Lynn Payer agrees that unnecessary testing is not worth the risks. While she recognizes the importance of early diagnosis of illness, she notes that many tests conducted today can be lethal. Angiography, for example, the examination of the coronary arteries by means of a catheter, leads to about one or two deaths for every 1,000 persons tested. A sampling of other high-risk tests she discusses in her book include the following.

High-Risk Medical Tests

Test	Reason	Possible Danger
Colonoscopy	Colon polyps	Colon perforation in 2 of every 10,000 subjects, Perforation then requires surgery with a 5 to 10 percent morbidity rate)
Investigation of biliary tract and pancreas	General disorders	Pancreatitis which is fatal in 2-5 percent of those affected
X-rays	Various	Small percentage experience allergic reaction which can result in death. In addition, x-ray exposure is cumulative; the more exposure, the greater risk of cancer

In addition, test results can lead to drugs which often create problems greater than the illness itself. Diagnoses for high cholesterol and high blood pressure are examples.[13]

Louise Lander, in her book *Defective Medicine,* believes that, "The initial, and most obvious problem is that medical science has not created anything resembling a mechanism for the systematic collection of data on any aspect of iatrogenic illness." She does admit that a system would be difficult to develop because an iatrogenic problem might not be obvious at first, might not be sourced easily and may appear in a delayed response.

A contributing factor to medicine's failure to systematically detect and track iatrogenesis is its tendency to stay away from issues of negligence and error in which the profession may be seen playing a significant role. A system to track medically induced injury and death would escalate the responsibility of malpractice. Turning a blind eye to this vital issue helps protect both medicine's power and its pocketbook.

Often people worry about dangers of major surgical procedures, not understanding that diagnostic tests can be just as risky.

Lander also takes a hard look at diagnostic techniques which carry risk to the patient, pointing out that any diagnostic technique that involves invading the body through drugs or instruments carries potential for harm. From anesthetizing and drugging the body to inserting tubes, needles and probes, to x-raying and cutting, the body's chance of being harmed or injured is always present. The risk, Landers states, grows geometrically when the patient "becomes the object of a whole smorgasbord of procedures..."

Lander cites one study of 198 patients who were victims of iatrogenesis at a prestigious teaching hospital, Yale's University Medical Service of Grace-New Haven Community Hospital. Of the 198 patients afflicted, 29 or 14.6 percent experienced problems resulting from diagnostic procedures or drugs used in diagnosing their problems. This represents 20 percent of hospital admissions during the time the study was conducted.[14]

Drugs have become a major source of iatrogenesis having come of age since the beginning of the twentieth century. In 1900 a physician had approximately six major forms of medication including digitalis, morphine, quinine, ether, diphtheria antitoxin and aspirin. A few immunizations were also available.[15]

Less than three quarters of a century later, the physician had almost 7,000 drugs to work with, more than 3,000 combinations of these drugs and more than 14,000 dosage forms and strengths, according to Lander's book citing Milton Silverman and Philip Lee's book, *Pills, Profits and Politics.*[16]

Each decade since the turn of the century has brought an increasing number of medications to the market. With such a vast number of pharmaceuticals at their disposal, doctors often rely on the information closest at hand to gain knowledge of drugs. Unfortunately much of this information is in varied forms of promotion or advertisement and originates from the drug manufacturers themselves. These promotions are often cleverly disguised as "reports," or "continuing education." To some, this method of "teaching" is a major problem with the legitimate drug market today. The "education" of doctors by pharmaceutical companies—the primary channel through which physicians gain their knowledge of drugs—is a central factor in the misuse and abuse of drugs and a major reason for the frequent implication of prescribed drugs in medically-induced illness and even death. When literature or training is presented by a pharmaceutical interest how objective can it be? How safe can it be?

An example of lack of objectivity and clear conflict of interest in the education of doctors is Ciba Geigy's role in the development of educational materials regarding children with ADD (Attention Deficit Disorder) or ADHD (Attention Deficit Hyperactivity Disorder) for which a common treatment is Ritalin (manufactured by Ciba Geigy). In a mid-1990's Public Broadcast special, investigators questioned the objectivity of Geigy's donation of more than $800,000 to C.H.A.D.D, a support organization directed toward parents of children with these disorders. C.H.A.D.D. literature demonstrated an overwhelming support for the use of Ritalin in spite of the drug's dangers, including addiction. In addition, a video supported financially by the United States Department of Education was shown to have a bias toward the use of Ritalin. If this criticism is justified, the government was helping Ciba Geigy sell Ritalin.

The overall picture is alarming, considering the incidence of in-bred healthcare and iatrogenic illness that results. Because of this, it is not surprising that the medical profession casts dispersions on other fields of health care, notably alternative methods, saying they are the systems to beware of. Andrew Weil points out traditional medicine argues against chiropractic treatment on the grounds that such treatment can cause stroke or paralysis.

Weil, a medical doctor by training but a practitioner who uses both alternative and allopathic methods as needed, points out that very few chiropractic adjustments over the past century have resulted in such incidences. He says, "Surely,...the AMA's accusation is a classic case of people in glass houses throwing stones." [17]

1. *Health and Healing,* Andrew Weil, MD, Houghton Mifflin, Boston, MA, Revised 1988 (pgs 96-102).

2. *Dissent in Medicine,* Robert S. Mendelsohn, MD et al, Contemporary Books, Chicago, IL, 1985, pgs. 79-82 (Mendelsohn also references Alan Scott Levin, M.D, "Corruption in American Medicine").

3. *The American Connection,* John Pekkanen, Chicago: Follett, 1973 (pp. 84-85).

4. "The Nature of Adverse Events in Hospitalized Patients," (Results of the Harvard Medical Practice Study II), L. Leape, MD, et al, *The New England Journal of Medicine,* Volume 324, #6, February 7, 1991.

5. *Health at the Crossroads,* Dean Black, Ph.D., Springville, UT: Springdale Press, 1988 Pgs 9-18).

6. *Defective Medicine,* Louise Lander, New York: Farrar, Straaus and Giroux.

7. *Health at the Crossroads,* Black, pg. 4.

8. "Chiropractors Speak Out Against Wall Street Journal's Distorted Diatribe," *The American Chiropractor,* May/June 1993.

9. *Confessions of a Medical Heretic,* Robert S. Mendelsohn, MD, 1980.

10. *The Great White Lie,* Walt Bogdanich, Touchstone: New York 1992, pg 73.

11. *Medication Errors: Causes and Prevention,* authors N.M. Davis and M.R. Cohen Philadelphia: George F. Stickley, 1981.

12. *Health and Healing,* Weil, pgs 93-95.

13. *The Disease Mongers,* Lynn Payer, John Wiley & Sons, 1992.

14. *Defective Medicine,* Lander.

15. "Chemical Intervention, " Sherman Mellinkoff, *Scientific American,* September '73, pg 103).

16. *Defective Medicine,* Lander.

17. *Health and Healing,* Weil, pg 94.

7

Women: The Captive Market

Forty million American women will go through menopause in the next two decades. In response, the North American Menopause Society discussed in a 1992 meeting how medical intervention might make this transition easier for women. Medical science had already decided decades earlier that a woman's body wasn't capable of handling menopause without intervention and that drugs were the way to go. The consensus at the 1992 meeting was that certain drugs would definitely make this life transition a better experience. In their estimation, not enough women were on estrogen replacement therapy. In fact only 15 percent of women going through menopause were on estrogen and the general feeling was that 95 percent of women could be "helped" by it.[1]

Sure there were risks—namely cancer—but a good number of the doctors felt the benefits outweighed the risks. These benefits included possible protection against osteoporosis, possible protection against heart disease, and perhaps assistance in improving memory.

Critics comment that while the medical community has decided to become fully involved in the menopause process, what they've really decided is how they can profit by it.

One opposing group goes beyond mild criticism to call the medical intervention of women at mid-life the "commercialization of menopause," accusing the medical community of manipulating a natural event in a woman's life in order to create a marketing opportunity for doctors and pharmaceutical companies at the expense of women's health.

Menopause has become feared because of the taboos society has placed on aging. The news media acts as the orchestra—playing out a stereotyping of women who happen to be making the transition from child-bearing to non-child bearing years. The media has played its part, but the menopause performance itself has been directed by another interest—the estrogen manufacturer as the orchestra's conductor. Unfortunately, this performance is rife with the discords of the unknown.

According to the Health Research Group (HRG), the Ralph Nader consumer advocacy branch of Public Citizen, the medical industry has re-worked menopause, has taken a normal body process and turned it into a disease. Medicine has convinced women that menopause is something that needs to be "taken care of," an illness that needs to be "cured." Medicine calls menopause a deficiency disease, namely, of the estrogen hormone.

In a 1991 presentation before the Senate Subcommittee on Aging, HRG expressed concern that drug companies have turned menopause into a billion-dollar money maker, treating it with a spectrum of prescription drugs. In this case, the money maker is hormone therapy, and the pricetag, HRG claims, is not just wasted money, but wasted health and even wasted life itself.

HRG pointed out that hormone replacement therapy (HRT)—the therapy used in menopause—is promoted to offer potential relief of the severe symptoms of menopause. These alleged benefits have been heavily marketed and include the hope of a reduction in the degen-

erative process of osteoporosis and assertions of a reduction in heart disease.

Yet, the downside is that the health benefits promised
have been overrated and the side effects of hormone therapy
inadequately communicated to the public.

Among these side effects is the risk of cancer, which
increased significantly in women during the 1970's. This
increased incidence of cancer has been associated with the
mass marketing of Premarin—the #1 best selling drug in
the United States—and other estrogens.

While results of studies point to the benefits of hormone therapy, HRG states that estrogen safety has
"never been documented in large, properly controlled and
randomized clinical trials." HRG's greatest concern is
the side effects.[2]

One 1991 report conducted by the Centers for Disease
Control (CDC) showed that their review of available literature demonstrated a close correlation between the length
of time a woman takes estrogen and her risk of cancer.

The authors of the CDC report looked at a number of
studies that measured the risk of breast cancer in estrogen
users. Their findings showed that women who take estrogen for more than 15 years increase their risk of breast
cancer by 30 percent, and when estrogen is taken over 25
years, there is a 50 percent increased risk.

Yet, the researchers noted a problem in the data they
examined. After categorizing all the studies by the quality of the epidemiological research (how well matched
the studies' subjects were—those who took estrogen and
did not get cancer compared to those who did take estrogen and developed cancer), the reviewers found a significant difference in the integrity of the data. The studies found to be of high quality showed the greatest increase in breast cancer. Low-to-medium quality tests
showed the least increase in cancer.

CDC reviewers then decided to isolate only the high
quality studies and examine their results separately in order to gain a more accurate perspective. What they found
was that instead of the 15-year estrogen user realizing a 30
percent increase in breast cancer incidence (as was determined when all studies were examined), the high quality

tests alone showed instead that the 15-year user had a 60 percent increased risk in cancer incidence and the 25-year estrogen user a 100 percent increased risk. The high quality tests showed that the risk of cancer due to taking estrogen actually doubled when compared to all tests of combined high, medium and low quality.[3]

In recent years, the belief that estrogen can help prevent heart disease has also been examined and the claim disputed. Dutch epidemiologists reported in 1994 that research asserting that women on HRT are 35-45 percent less likely to die from heart disease is inaccurate. What is true is that women on HRT are generally healthier women because of a higher financial status (they can afford a healthier lifestyle) compared to those less healthy with less healthy lifestyles who, in addition, cannot afford the drug. They concluded that existing studies showing that estrogen aids heart disease prevention are weak.[4]

The results of the Dutch study support an earlier study cited in a 1991 edition of the *Journal of the American Medical Association* stating that women taking estrogen are usually white, educated, upper middle class and lean. Their incidence of heart disease has already been lessened by the general state of their health before they begin hormone replacement therapy.[5]

Proponents of estrogen therapy maintained that estrogen therapy was a factor in the lessened incidence of heart disease when, in fact, the women were generally healthy before taking estrogen and probably would not have experienced heart disease with any greater frequency without hormone therapy.

Test results showing estrogen's effects on heart disease have flip-flopped over the past thirty years depending on what interest group was backing the particular study. In the 1960's, a number of researchers reported that estrogen was the premier protection against a number of ailments associated with aging, including cardiovascular disease. Then, in the 1970's, studies published in the United States began raising doubts about the drug's effects.

A number of these studies showed that estrogen can actually increase the risk of cardiovascular disease, according to doctors in the Netherlands who have continuously examined studies on estrogen.[6]

As far back as 1975, Nader's Health Research Group warned the FDA about the effects of estrogen usage pointing to evidence dating back to the 1930s of their cancer-causing properties and asking for a review of the risks and benefits of the drug and their indiscriminate prescribing.

Citing a State of Washington survey and extrapolating it to include the entire country, HRG estimated that an estimated 22 million prescriptions were being written for women whose doctors thought they should be on hormone therapy. The conditions for which estrogen was prescribed included mental disorders, senility, disease of bones and organs and other conditions. HRG's conclusion was that the treatment of these ailments with estrogen was at best, "questionably effective," especially where there was no evidence that the applications had met any standards for efficacy.

HRG claimed that more than 75 percent of all prescriptions written for these drugs were not warranted, either because their efficacy had not been proven or because the benefits were minimal in comparison to the risk of cancer.

The warnings were there, yet millions of women were being prescribed estrogen substances such as Premarin (the most dispensed drug in the United States), and a good proportion of these women were taking estrogen for a period of years. The Washington study noted that the median length of usage in the mid-70's was 10 years.

HRG blames Ayerst and other drug companies for taking advantage of physicians as well as millions of American women by creating the illusion that these women were lacking in some chemical, that they were abnormal and doing themselves a great disservice if they did not take estrogen therapy. By extension, doctors were made to feel they, too, were abnormal if they did not prescribe estrogen.[7]

According to HRG, the majority of prescriptions written to offset problems of menopause come with the risk of cancer. The benefits, HRG states, are "trivial in comparison to the risk of cancer."

When the evidence of risk could no longer be ignored, drug companies began adding progestins to the estrogen; supposedly to help offset the cancer risk. Even so, the FDA reported the following in its June 1986 drug bulletin:

> [The] FDA recently recommended to estrogen
> manufacturers that they also note in their
> estrogen labeling that studies have shown the
> addition of a progestin for seven or more days of
> an estrogen cycle is associated with a lower
> incidence of endometrial hyperplasia than an
> estrogen-only cycle. Morphological and
> biochemical studies of the endometrium suggest
> that 10 to 13 days of progestin are needed to
> provide maximal maturation of the endometrium
> and eliminate any hyperplastic changes. Whether
> this will provide protection from endometrial
> carcinoma has not been clearly established.
> Possible additional risks that may be associated
> with the inclusion of progestin in estrogen
> replacement therapy include effects on
> carbohydrate and lipid metabolism.[8]

Estrogen evidently affects carbohydrate and lipid metabolism to increase cholesterol levels, which, in addition
to related risks, can contribute to the risk of heart disease.
Women who are taking estrogen with progestin added in
the revised "safer" formulation in order to help prevent heart
disease might be *increasing* their chances of heart disease.

In a May 1984 letter to Mark Novitch, MD, the acting
commissioner of the FDA, HRG addressed the issue of other
types of estrogen risks including congenital birth defects,
including passing on congenital heart defects and limb reduction in women using hormone-based oral contraceptives.
One study was cited estimating an almost five-fold increase
in limb reduction in infants exposed in utero to sex hormones including contraceptives, hormone withdrawal tests
for pregnancy or treatment for threatened abortion. Expo-
sures included both long- and short-term treatment. The
letter from Nader's Health Research Group (HRG) to the
FDA Commissioner appealed for greater warnings to the
patient about the effects of hormones on the body.[9]

HRG officials had no illusions that they would be successful in eliminating estrogen from drugstore shelves. The
goal was to urge the FDA to require that estrogen manufacturers provide stronger labeling and packaging warnings advising those who take the drug of cancer risks, birth
abnormalities and other suspected side effects instead of
allowing drug manufacturers to bury warnings in the

physician's guidelines or omit them entirely. HRG also pushed for a requirement that women sign a consent form acknowledging that they are aware of the potential negative effects of the product when they receive a prescription.

In a January 1989 statement, HRG requested the following be included in both information to the doctor and the patient as well:

> **Despite a number of earlier and more recent studies which found no link between use of the pill and breast cancer, six studies in women in the last seven years, four in the last two years, have shown an association between the use of oral contraceptives and breast cancer in women whose diagnosis of breast cancer was made before the age of 45.**[10]

A revision made in August of 1992 was required for patient package inserts for estrogen products including Hormone Replacement Therapy (HRT) and birth control. Among the warnings in this revision:

1. Warning of uterine cancer for women who have experienced menopause; breast cancer warning;

2. Warning that women should not take estrogen during pregnancy due to the risk of miscarriage and birth defect, and estrogen should not be used until after a woman stops breast feeding;

3. Warning that women who have had cancer increase their risk of additional cancer by taking estrogen;

4. Warning that women with circulation problems should not take estrogen due to the risk of blood clots;

5. Warning that taking estrogen following menopause increases a woman's likelihood of developing gall bladder disease;

6. Warning that benign tumors of the uterus might enlarge with estrogen use;

7. Warning of possible skin discoloration which might indicate liver complication.

8. Warning that estrogen usage might cause nausea and vomiting as well as breast tenderness and enlargement.

9. Warning of fluid retention potential which might
worsen some conditions such as asthma, epilepsy,
migraine, kidney disease and heart disease.

10. Note that estrogen does not work to offset
depression or nervousness. It also has not been
proven that estrogen assists in keeping the skin
youthful or helps maintain the feeling of youth. Only
women likely to develop osteoporosis should use
estrogen as hormone replacement therapy.[11]

The FDA guidelines that estrogen manufacturers must
use in their package insert mention that studies are not
conclusive regarding the risks of taking estrogen-based
drugs. The effect of this comment as well as news of conflicting studies confuse both patients and doctors.

It is, however, apparent to many that the risks of taking estrogen far outweigh any benefits which may or may
not exist with hormone use.

To millions of women birth control is the all-important
benefit of estrogen. Especially for the young whose concern
over illness and mortality frequently has not yet matured,
birth control is so much desired that the negative potential
of estrogen is not considered.

In recognition of this trend, HRG went beyond their
concern for communicating specific risks of estrogen usage
to patients, focusing efforts on high dosage birth control
with strengths of more than 50 ug (micrograms). Their literature points out that the National Prescription Audit
(NPA) indicated that almost 4 percent of prescriptions in
1986 were for pills with more than 50 ug, meaning that
250,000 women were taking the high dose pills out of 7.3
million taking the pill, and 25.5 percent or 1.87 million
women were using 50 ug dosage pills. Lowering the dosage
reduces only the risks which include blood clots, heart disease, cancer; it does not eliminate them.

Studies cited in Public Citizen publication #1116 point
to increased risks with high dosage birth control:

Risks with High Dosage Birth Control Pills

Blood Clots

Birth control pills containing from 100-150 ug of estrogen associated with 2- 3 times more risk than those pills 50 ug or less.

Heart Attacks

High dose birth control pills (100 to 150 ug) associated with increased risk of atherosclerotic heart disease and subsequent myocardial infarction or stroke (risk related to both estrogen and progestogen content).

Breast/Cervical Cancer

Two-fold increase in breast cancer when using birth control with 50ug or more of estrogen in women using the pill one to four years before first term pregnancy, and birth control creates a two-fold risk of cervical cancer. Long-term users have an even greater risk of cervical cancer.

HRG has cited findings from the 1960s demonstrating a suspected tie between estrogen and cancer and estrogen and other life-threatening illnesses. In spite of this, the United States lagged behind Sweden, England and other countries in moving toward a reduction in estrogen levels in drugs.[12]

The Pill made its debut in 1960. Its onset was celebrated as a major medical achievement that would change family life and social life in general. It did. According to an article in the *FDA Consumer* that appeared in 1990, women readily accepted the new medication and sales grew quickly in the United States. By the early 1980s about 10 million women were using the Pill in the U.S. After concerns were made public regarding the safety of the Pill, prescriptions dropped to 8.4 million.[13]

Negative reports about the Pill began as early as 1961 in the United States and England. Studies pointed to serious side effects including heart attack and stroke. Over the next few years, reports of side effects continued but it wasn't until four years later, in 1965, that the FDA finally acted on these concerns by contracting a scientist at Johns Hopkins School of Hygiene and Public Health to look into the reports. The FDA also formed the Advisory Committee on Obstetrics to examine the

Pill's role in side effects, especially those related to breast, cervical and endometrial cancer.

In 1966, the advisory committee reported that it had found "no scientific data, at this time, to prove the pill unsafe for human use." As far as cancer was concerned, the committee said it would take years before the Pill's role could be assessed. The World Health Organization said that its findings concurred with those of the committee. Meanwhile, doctors continued prescribing a drug suspected of being a deadly risk to millions of women.

Meanwhile, research in England demonstrated a definite increase in blood clots among women taking the pill. Because of this, in 1969 the British Committee on Safety of Drugs recommended that oral contraceptives with more than 50 ug (micrograms) of estrogen not be prescribed. The British Committee's recommendation led to the virtual disappearance of high estrogen pills in England after 1970.[14]

With more conclusive evidence coming to light, the FDA had no choice but to make a move, but instead of acting quickly as was the case in England, the FDA issued directives to pharmaceutical companies requiring them to add the evidence from British studies to oral contraceptive package labeling. Later warnings from U.S. studies that supported the British research were added to the labeling. By 1969, 7.5 million women in the U.S. were taking oral contraceptives and even though so many women might be risking their health, even their lives, it wasn't until the early 1970's that the FDA began *encouraging* doctors to heed warnings about high estrogen prescriptions, and to use lower dosages when possible. The warnings were accompanied by product labeling revisions and, for the first time, package warnings directed to the patient.[15]

In the mid 1970s lower dose oral contraceptives (50mcg or less) were being taken by most women. Nevertheless, in 1986, 3.4 percent of all women taking the Pill were still on high dose oral contraceptives. While 3.4 percent may seem like an insignificant number, it accounted for 400,000 women.

It wasn't until 1988 at the FDA's urging and following a lengthy appeal by Public Citizen to the FDA regarding the dangers of the high estrogen Pill, that the three drug companies still manufacturing high-dose estrogen oral contraceptives "voluntarily" withdrew their products—almost twenty years after the withdrawal of the product in England.[16]

Today the FDA and pharmaceutical manufacturers pat themselves on the back for their reduction of both estrogen and progestin content. According to FDA's *Consumer Magazine*, estrogen content in oral contraceptives is now generally one third of what the early Pill contained, and the progestin content is approximately one tenth or less of what it was in the early years.

The typical prescription for the Pill in the 1960s was for 100-150 mcg of estrogen; in the 1970s, the typical prescription was 50mcg or less. In the 1980s and 1990s, prescriptions are typically written in the 30-35 mcg range. This amounts to thirty years of experimenting on the wrong side of the drug approval process, and still the question remains, "Is it safe?"

The FDA admits to the possibility of side effects, observing that the risks have decreased along with the decrease in estrogen/progestin levels for healthy, non-smoking women although there is a "slightly increased" risk of cardiovascular disease for women who smoke, according to Philip Corfman MD of the FDA's metabolism and endocrine drug product division. Yet the FDA also is quick to point out the *alleged* "benefits" which include a decreased incidence of endometrial cancer, benign cysts of the ovaries and inflammatory disease of the breasts and pelvis.[17]

While it is conceded that the presence of estrogen and/or progestins in the Pill might increase cardiovascular disease, in menopausal women estrogen is supposed to help reduce cardiovascular disease (a primary reason for taking it). Confusion also exists interpreting the incidence of cancer related to estrogen. The FDA touts the benefits women can derive from the Pill, including a decrease in the incidence of certain forms of cancer. Yet estrogen has been blamed for contributing to cancer in women on hormone therapy for menopause. The average non-medical person is confused about how estrogen can cause cancer in menopausal women, yet hinder its development in oral contraceptive users. The question is also raised: How can estrogen create a greater risk of cardiovascular disease in oral contraceptive users and hinder cardiovascular development in menopausal women? The confusion keeps women in the dark regarding the truth about estrogen drugs.

Also confusing is an FDA comment that the health benefits of the Pill are associated with the 50 ug dosages of estrogen. If so, how can estrogen at higher dosages both cause and help prevent heart disease? And how can estrogen at higher dosages both cause and prevent cancer?

In the FDA's publication, "The Pill, 30 Years of Safety Concerns," one column notes the health benefits of oral contraceptives including a decrease in ovarian and endometrial cancers, benign cysts of the ovaries and breasts and pelvic inflammatory disease. Two columns later (and on the same page), the statement reads, "Uncertainties remain about whether the pill causes breast or cervical cancer in some groups of women." Perhaps it ultimately comes down to a woman deciding to make herself vulnerable to any risk at all whatever those risks might be.

A similar contradiction exists in "Estrogens," an FDA article from 1990. On the bottom of one page, the writer describes how large doses of estrogen (30 mgs daily) might be used to treat breast cancer. In the next column the section reads, "It's unknown whether estrogen use increases a woman's risk of breast cancer." The reader wonders how estrogen can both help in the treatment and contribute to the disease, in this case breast cancer.[18]

The research does say that estrogens might help treat some cancers and increase the risks of others and that certain age groups might be more susceptible to certain cancers if estrogen is taken. For example, menopausal women might be more inclined to develop endometrial cancer if taking estrogen over a long period of time. Yet, because research is insubstantial and the reports often contradictory, the "causes" and "cures" are closer to guesses than fact.

Dr. Corfman, who served in the FDA's division of metabolism and endocrine drug products, was quoted in "The Pill," an FDA reprint, saying he believes that even if there are risks with oral contraceptives, the health benefits outweigh them for most women. Concerned members of the public reply, "But no one knows what the actual risks are. Medical research is not consistent. The reports continue to show a high degree of conflicting evidence."

Corfman also said that of the studies to date (December, 1990) all research had been done only on higher-dose pills (50ug or more). No studies had been done on the lower dosage pills and to his knowledge, none were underway. His general sentiment was that more studies were needed.

Howard Shapiro, MD, in his work, *The New Birth-Control Book*, stated that in the late 1980's, approximately 12 percent of all women on the Pill were on dosages of 0.050 milligrams of estrogen. This compares with a 1985 study, when 30 percent of oral contraceptive users were found to be taking dosages of 0.050 milligrams or more. These higher dosages were being taken even when lower, safer preparations were readily available. While in his estimation, the risks were relatively low in almost all age groups, Shapiro was concerned about those women in the highest risk group, age 35 and over, women who were "five times as likely to be taking a high-dose pill as women in the youngest age group (15 to19 years of age).

In his explanations of the dangers of using the Pill, Shapiro primarily points to the risk of heart attack and stroke and other related problems such as pulmonary embolism and blood clots rather than cancer.[19]

It appears that the risks have scared many away from the Pill over the years, particular for women in specific risk categories: smokers, obese women, women who have heart-related conditions, liver or cancer history, and those over 40 as Dr. Shapiro notes. Yet one of the most recent developments in the Pill's 30-plus year history is the FDA's approval in 1989 for use in healthy, non-smoking women over 40 years of age. The move was anticipated to add 1 to 1.5 million users to the oral contraceptive roles. More drug use means more money. The greater the market, the more profitable the drug.

When critics ask, "Who is leading whom?" they are asking, "Is the FDA leading the pharmaceutical companies or are the pharmaceutical companies leading the FDA?" The FDA seems to enjoy maintaining open markets for drugs once they have been approved but takes a dangerously long time to react to reports of their adverse effects. Certainly this is not at the expense of the drug companies. The expense is paid by the public.

The bottom line is that there is no definitive answer for women who are trying to decide whether estrogen—in any form—is the right choice for them. Because there is no conclusive research on safety or the lack of it, there is only personal choice, and that choice ultimately comes down to whether a woman is willing to take the risks that are an unavoidable partner in estrogen therapy, in birth control, in estrogen use in any form. Each woman must weigh the benefits as well as the risks for herself. Each woman must ask herself if estrogen is worth the price she may have to pay, even if that price—perhaps—is her life.

1. "At Third Meeting, Menopause Experts Make the Most of Insufficient Data," Medical News and Perspectives, by Andrew A. Skolnick, v268, *JAMA, The Journal of the American Medical Association,* November 11, 1992, p2483(3).

2. Public Citizen Health Research Group Testimony before the Senate Subcommittee on Aging, Hearing on the Role of Menopause and Gender Differences in Aging on the Development of Disease in Mid-Life and Older Women, April 19, 1991, (transcript written in HRG Publication #1220).

3. HRG Publication #1220.

4. *Harvard Health Letter,* Nov. 1994 v 20 n1 page 8.

5. *JAMA, The Journal of the American Medical Association,* April 10, 1991.

6. *Lancet,* April 6, 1991, 833-4.

7. Public Citizen's Health Research Group to FDA Advisory Committee on the Use of Estrogens During Menopause, December 16, 1975.

8. *FDA Drug Bulletin,* June 1986, Volume 16 Number 1.

9. Health Resource Group Letter to Mark Novitch, MD, Acting Commissioner, FDA, May 23, 1984.

10. Statement by Public Citizen, Health Research Group director, on the need for immediate revision of doctor and patient labeling for the birth control pill, January 1989.

11. FDA Labeling Guidance for Estrogen Drug Products, Patient Package Insert, Revised 1992.

12. Public Citizen Health Research Group statement during the FDA Workshop on Birth Control with an Estrogen Content Greater Than 50 Micrograms, January 15, 1988. Transcript of the workshop shown in HRG publication #1116.

13. "The Pill, 30 Years of Safety Concerns," by Sharon Snider, reprint from the *FDA Consumer Magazine,* December 1990.

14. "Thromboembolism, Cancer and Oral Contraceptives," M. Vessey, *Clinic Ob Gyn* 1974 17(1): 65.

15. "The Pill," *FDA Consumer* reprint, December 1990.

16. "The Pill," *FDA Consumer,* reprint, 1990.

17. "The Pill," *FDA Consumer* reprint, 1990.

18. "Estrogens," How to Take Your Medicine, reprint from the *FDA Consumer,* November 1990.

19. *The New Birth-Control Book,* Howard Shapiro, Prentice Hall Press, 1988.

8

Medicating the Child

We try to teach our children that street drugs are wrong...that crack, marijuana, speed and all the others are dangerous, illegal. We preach to them that drugs can kill, that at the very least, drugs can do irreparable harm. Yet, through our own actions, through our own use of painkillers, tranquilizers, a drug for this and a drug for that—a drug for whatever ails us, we confuse our kids. We confuse them by saying that some drugs—specifically our drugs—are okay, and so are those drugs we ourselves decide our kids should have because our doctor told us as parents these drugs are good.

The dogma is that medical drugs are okay because they are legal. Yet, how many people have been addicted to legal drugs, hurt by them, their lives destroyed by them, even killed by them? How many painkillers, tranquilizers, drugs—any number of drugs—work to mask a person's symptoms, but do not get to the real solution—building better health? It's clearly a double standard that legal drugs are okay, but illegal ones aren't. Both can and are often dangerous.

What is the real difference between a legal pill that makes us feel better or safe, and an illegal one that makes us feel better or safe? Every drug—legal and illegal alike— is toxic. But there is one important difference. The legal pill comes with a prescription written by society's God, a doctor, who in turn is groomed by one of the most lucrative industries in the world. Is it any wonder this industry is so profitable when the medical world believes that good health comes in the shape of a medicine bottle? Maybe the pharmaceutical industry has the majority of us fooled, but not all of us. We can realize as intelligent human beings that although a few drugs may be therapeutic, drugs—all drugs—can be dangerous, even deadly.

Perhaps one day the majority of us will realize that drugs—licit and illicit—are not the answer to feeling better or the path to better health. With that understanding, we'll realize that the "war on drugs" should be pointed in more than one direction.

The idea that pharmaceutical drugs can be classified along with illegal drugs as potentially "bad" is a concept few people have considered. While some legal drugs can be therapeutic, many have been known to have even greater destructive powers. There is a fine line between those that are therapeutic and those that are dangerous, between those that are good and those that are bad.

Through the mass marketing of pharmaceutical products, the legal drug industry would like to ensure profits by keeping the public on a steady diet of pills, capsules and liquids from birth through death. The best way to accomplish this is by constantly creating new reasons for the public to take drugs while playing down the risks. The industry must encourage people to believe that drugs are rarely bad (dangerous), that mostly they are good (therapeutic) and that drugs are the way to better health. When marketing drugs for children, the safety element is particularly important, yet too often circumvented.

The "early years" marketing technique used is not unlike teaching a child to read: introduce the child to reading in a positive way, make reading a daily activity, a way of life, and the young person will become a lifelong reader.

With pharmaceutical products, the conditioning works much the same way. Teach a child (through his parents)to take a drug for every ache, pain, cold, sleepless night, moment of depression, fever, ailment, and for every disease he might contract. In this way a customer, a lifelong customer, is made.

The pharmaceutical industry holds the customer's health in its hands. It owes the public more than a well-marketed, well-packaged product. Drugs are toxic, and their potential danger cannot be dismissed no matter what their alleged therapeutic benefits might be.

For children, drug dangers begin before birth including drugs given the mother for conditions including morning sickness, pain, water weight as well as drugs given to expedite the birth process. Each drug the fetus is exposed to creates an environment of possible injury. Potential dangers continue with the process of immunizing which begins virtually from birth. These childhood shots earn the position as both the most highly promoted children's medication as well as the primary way most children are ushered into the vast cornucopia of pharmaceutical products with the full cooperation of parents, community, schools, and government.

Parents are led to believe that immunizations protect children from diseases including polio, diphtheria, pertussis, measles, and a number of other infectious diseases which medicine tells us will be prevented if children are immunized. "Without it," the billboard and television ads warn, "they don't stand a chance." "Protect our nation's future. Immunize." For parents, the television, radio and print ads say that vaccinations are their children's only hope for a bright future, a healthy one. The ads scream negligence if parents don't "protect" their kids by immunizing them, that they are bad parents. These techniques compel parents to action.

Yet those who will listen can hear a warning that the ads are not necessarily born out of a sincere concern for our children, that protecting the nation's youth isn't the primary intention of those who promote immunizations. Instead, these warning voices say, such messages are motivated by the prospects of profits to be made from instilling fear in the minds of parents who learn to fear that their child might get polio from a classmate's coughing on them or whooping cough from drinking out of a water fountain. Instilling fear is the vaccine promoters' means to an end.

Fear is a powerful motivation. It encourages people to take action when they otherwise might not. Consider bomb shelters and the Communist scare in the 1950s. Think about the ignorant fear many have over associating with those infected with HIV. Fear causes people to act irrationally, to follow the crowd. In the case of vaccines, fear makes money for pharmaceutical companies and physicians while placing our children at risk.

The dark side of profits cannot be dismissed lightly because it explains why medicine chooses to be invasive, chooses to intervene when "less might be more," when not invading, not interfering, might be the best choice.

The lure of profits from vaccinations lurks in a prominent feature on the walls of the treatment rooms of many pediatric offices: the schedule for childhood immunizations. Like most pediatric offices, Pediatrics, P.C. in Kalamazoo, Michigan, posts a standard immunization schedule for children: 2 months of age, 4 months, 6 months, 9 months, 15 months, 18 months 24 months, 5 years, 11 years, 14 and 17 years, for a total billing of $565 just for the vaccinations. Regular office visits where vaccinations are administered range from $35-$55 per visit and add a minimum of $600 in fees. This is above and beyond emergency visits for colds, flu and allergies and other medical conditions.[1]

Without providing immunizations and antibiotics, most pediatricians' practices would find their profitability compromised. These two forms of treatment help ensure a doctor's financial success. Yet there's more that points to an extraordinary greed. For example, in order to enhance their income, many doctors have adopted a practice called the "vaccination half-dose," which requires a first visit for a vaccination, then a follow-up visit for the completion of the same immunization. This amounts to virtually a doubling of costs under the guise that half-doses are easier on the child's health, resulting in an additional fee for both the vaccination and the visit. Yet, expense is secondary to another danger—the risk of severe reaction and sometimes even death to the children who are administered these drugs.

In the publication *American Chiropractor,* a nurse writes to columnist Ted Koren, D.C.:

> I am a coordinator for a childhood immunization clinic. We often see small children who have had their shots at physicians' offices. How do you explain repeated visits at 15 days' intervals with half doses? That's more than 20 visits before the age of two for immunizations alone. Costly for parents, but lucrative for the physicians. And that does not take into account the fact that half doses are not recommended by the CDC [Centers for Disease Control].

Harris Coulter, PhD, has written extensively on the abuses of the pharmaceutical industry including the work, *Vaccination, Social Violence and Criminality,* an expose' on vaccination abuse; as well as *The Controlled Clinical Trial,* a critical look at modern medicine's drug testing process. Coulter believes, "Half doses are more dangerous for the child because of the repeated stresses on the immune system."[2]

The dangers exist in particular for seven of the most common vaccinations whether given in half or full doses: polio, diphtheria, measles, German measles (Rubella), mumps, tetanus and pertussis (whooping cough).

Immunizations don't guarantee a child won't contract the disease the vaccination is designed to prevent. In some cases, in fact, parents who insist on immunizations may be exposing the child to an increased risk of contracting that disease. Immunizations can also leave a child vulnerable to a wide assortment of other side effects, many of which have been known to leave permanent damage, sometimes death.

Even if the medically-influenced media were to report cases of vaccination side effects, accurate statistics are not readily available since only 10 percent of doctors bother to report them to the centralized Vaccine Adverse Events Reporting System (VAERS) currently in place. Even more frightening is the fact that most adverse reactions aren't readily linked or admitted to as the probable effect of the vaccination itself, according to Barbara Loe Fisher, co-founder and president of the National Vaccine Information Center.[3]

The generally accepted viewpoint that vaccinations do more good than harm is biased, according to Fisher, especially the myth that vaccinations have virtually wiped out certain dreaded diseases. Many experts say that instead, the incidence of many diseases was already on a decline before vaccinations were introduced. Most diseases appear, peak and wane at their own pace.

In his book *Medical Nemesis*, social critic Ivan Illich notes that:

> In New York in 1812, the death rate [from tuberculosis] was estimated to be higher than 700 per 10,000; by 1882, when Koch first isolated and cultured the bacillus, it had already declined to 370 per 10,000. The rate was down to 180 when the first sanitorium opened in 1910....Cholera, dysentery, and typhoid similarly peaked and dwindled outside the physician's control....The combined death rate from scarlet fever, diphtheria, whooping cough and measles among children up to fifteen shows that nearly 90 percent of the total decline in mortality between 1860-1965 had occurred before the introduction of antibiotics and wide-spread immunization.[4]

For example, between 1923 and 1953, before Jonas Salk's killed-virus polio vaccine was introduced, the rate of polio in the United States and England had already declined by approximately 50 percent. This trend was also repeated in other European countries. Following Salk's 1955 development of the killed virus vaccine, many countries in Europe decided against mass immunizations. The epidemic continued to decline there as well as in countries conducting mass immunizations, according to Neil Miller in his book *Vaccines: Are They Really Safe and Effective?*

Miller's figures agree with those reported in Illich's book and specifically show the following declines in U.S. death rates for several illnesses:

Diseases Declining Before
Introduction of Vaccine

Pre-Vaccine

Disease	Decline Period	% decline*	Year of vaccine
Polio	1923-53	47%	1955 (killed virus)
			1959 (live virus)
Diphtheria	1900-1930	90%	Late 1930s
Measles	1915-1958	95%	Early 1960s
Pertussis	1900-1935	75%	Late 1930s

Percentage decrease from greatest number of reported cases

Miller also shows that in the case of smallpox, the highest death rate in England for any two-year period before the compulsory vaccination law of 1853 was 2,000, but after more than fifteen years of mandatory smallpox vaccine, more than 23,000 people died of the disease in 1870-71 alone. Deaths from smallpox fell only after immunizations for smallpox diminished. In 1881, 96.5 percent of infants in England and Wales were vaccinated, and smallpox deaths reached 3,708 per million population. In 1941, when less than 40 percent of babies were administered the vaccine, death from smallpox had diminished to 1 death per million. Miller's book cites case after case of studies that correlate the high incidence of contracting smallpox with those who have been vaccinated for the disease.[5]

Citing a study conducted by the World Health Organization in 1968, Illich writes that improved nutrition, not vaccinations, was the primary reason for the decline in these illnesses since good nutrition creates higher host-resistance to disease:

> In poor countries today, diarrhea and upper-
> respiratory-tract infections occur more frequently,
> last longer, and lead to higher mortality where

nutrition is poor, no matter how much or how
little medical care is available....For more than a
century, analysis of disease trends has shown that
the environment is the primary determinant of the
state of general health of any population.[6]

Evidence that vaccinations do not prevent and can actually cause the diseases they are designed to prevent is
illustrated below:

Illnesses Caused by or Connected to Vaccines

Illness	% of Cases	Time Span
Polio	87%	1973-1983 (Except imported cases)—U.S. Dept of Health & Human Services
	100%	1980-1989 (Except imported cases)—Centers for Disease Control
Measles	58%	1984 (school-age children)
Pertussis	46%*	All U.S. children 7 months to 6 years of age who contracted the disease in 1984
Smallpox	90%*	Late 1800s

*Vaccinated cases

Cases cited taken from *Vaccines: Are They Really Safe and Effective?*

Miller also points out that the incidence of polio cases
actually increased following mass immunizations in the mid
1950s. Before mass immunizations, Massachusetts reported
273 cases of poliomyelitis and 2,027 following immunization.
Rhode Island reported 22 cases before and 122 after, while
New Hampshire reported 38 cases before and 129 after.

Even though there was a growing body of evidence that
the drug was ineffective as well as unsafe, Miller states
that the United States Public Health Service signed a proc-
lamation saying that the polio vaccine was 100 percent safe
and effective, no doubt persuaded by the vaccine manufacturer Parke-Davis. Then, as the incidence of polio continued to climb following the introduction of the polio vaccine,

the disease itself was redefined making cases difficult to track. By making the definition of polio much more specific, other illnesses which had previously been defined as "polio" were deleted. As a result, it appeared that fewer people had contracted the illness. This is one way health authorities can skew numbers in order for a vaccine to appear less dangerous. According to Miller:

> The practice of redefining a disease when it is contracted by an "immunized" person is not new. This was a common tactic during the smallpox epidemics as well. For example, in 1936 in Great Britain the Ministry of Health admitted that the vaccine status of the individual is a guiding factor in diagnosis. In other words, if a person who is vaccinated contracts the disease, the disease is simply recorded under a different name.

In addition to redefining a disease following the onset of mass vaccination for it, immunization proponents also recorded the effects of the vaccination in a way to support its existing and continued use. For example, antibody levels (in many cases) were measured instead of examining actual infection rates; the latter would be more damaging to the cause for vaccinations.[7]

The fact that vaccines have been known to cause serious side effects as well as the very illness they are intended to prevent and even death have been well documented.

Research scientist Viera Schiebner, Ph.D, in her book *Vaccination: The Medical Assault on The Immune System,* explains that after reviewing more than 30,000 pages of medical studies, she discovered a significant increase in the incidence of crib death (SIDS) following infant vaccination. When she attempted to alert authorities of her findings, her words fell upon deaf ears.[8]

Harris Coulter, Ph.D., medical historian, in his book *Vaccination, Social Violence and Criminality*, documents that vaccines can damage a child throughout life causing problems such as autism, hyperactivity, attention deficit disorders (ADD), dyslexia, allergies and a host of other problems that rarely existed before the onset of mass vaccination programs. He focuses on evidence that vaccinations can also lead to social maladjustment.[9]

In recent years, noted side effects have been connected with the vaccine given for Pertussis (whooping cough), and also with vaccines given to prevent measles/mumps/rubella (MMR) and polio, the vaccine known as OPV or oral polio vaccine.

In a brochure distributed by the National Vaccine Information Center (NVIC) in Vienna, Virginia, a number of children are pictured who experienced violent reactions to immunizations. The brochure tells a brief story for each of them:

Anna

Within two days of receiving her first MMR shot at 15 months of age, Anna began limping. During the next two weeks, she stopped walking, developed unusual cold symptoms, fever and irritability, and wanted to be held constantly. During the following six weeks, she became totally paralyzed and at three years, Anna could not walk or talk. She remains severely handicapped.

Ashley

After her fourth DPT shot as well as OPV and HIB [influenza] vaccines, Ashley experienced a severe reaction within 72 hours including a high fever, lethargy and was hospitalized with kidney failure and encephalitis. She remains severely handicapped, mentally and physically.

Kimberlie

Kimberlie was two months old when she received her first DPT and OPV vaccines. Within three hours, she ran a high fever, began screaming and went into convulsions. She died of cardiac arrest.

Joshua

At six months of age, Joshua had his third DPT and OPV shots. Within six hours he began screaming, did not want to be comforted, ran a fever and lapsed into a *grand mal* seizure. Today he is classified as moderately to severely mentally retarded.[10]

Medical experts usually counter reports of severe vaccination reaction by asserting that they are extremely rare or that the reactions cannot be directly linked to the vaccination. Yet when parents note over and over again the effects their children experience following vaccination, mere "coincidence" is not a rational conclusion. When there appears no other logical causal factor, the likely and logical deduction must be that vaccinations cause many children to react. In many cases, that reaction ends in permanent damage and even death.

Vaccination reactions are not as rare as vaccination proponents would like the public to believe. In the same brochure, "They Had No Voice. They Had No Choice" is the following:

> Most parents don't know that the pertussis
> (whooping cough) portion of the DPT shot can
> cause convulsions, shock, brain inflammation, and
> death within hours or days of the vaccination. One
> large U.S. study found that one in 875 DPT shots
> produces a convulsion or collapse/shock reaction,
> which means some 18,000 DPT shots cause
> American children to suffer one of these
> neurological reactions every year.

The measles/mumps/rubella (MMR) shot can cause brain inflammation and death. NVIC literature states that in a U.S. study, a relationship between the rubella vaccine and chronic arthritis has been discovered. Various disorders of the nervous system and the blood have also been linked to this vaccine. Adult women who have had the rubella vaccine have been found to experience a higher rate of joint problems, including arthritis.

Finally, the oral polio vaccine (OPV) has been known to cause encephalitis, death and, ironically, polio in the shot's recipient as well as in those who come in close contact with that recipient.[11]

NVIC notes that more than 54,000 adverse reactions following vaccinations including convulsions, brain swelling and even death were reported to the government spanning a three-year period which ended in October of 1993. However, since only an estimated 10 percent of injuries is reported, and there is even less follow up to determine possible serious reactions to immunizations, this figure is only a fraction of what is actually occurring to children and adults across America.

For parents who understand the potential dangers involved with childhood immunizations, many states offer religious or philosophical exemptions, while all 50 states offer medical exemptions. Still, according to NVIC, "Many state legislators are being urged by federal health officials and medical organizations, to revoke this exemption to vaccination."[12] Unfortunately, as vaccines become increasingly mandatory, we lose even more control over a health decision that should be our own to make. It wouldn't be so difficult to accept mandatory vaccinations if the result were positive, but at every turn, that decision is made for us. Big business is the winner. The public pays with compromised health—or worse.

To demonstrate the government's diminishing concern over the dangers of vaccinations, U.S. Health and Human Services Secretary Donna Shalala laid out the final rules of the 1986 National Childhood Vaccine Injury Act. (From 1986 to 1993 the federal compensation program had awarded nearly $400 million to 1,000 families of children injured or killed by vaccines.) Shalala's guidelines have drastically reduced which children can be compensated following alleged injury by the DPT vaccine.

NVIC reported in their March 1995 newsletter, *The Vaccine Reaction:*

> **One lawyer who represents vaccine injured children in the U.S. Court of Claims, commented, "What you have now can be compared to a federal program that will compensate anyone who is in a plane crash in a snow storm within 10 miles of Tahiti. Nobody will ever qualify."**[13]

NVIC serves as a clearinghouse for information that, they, and not the federal government, make available to concerned parents and others. The address for the organization is: National Vaccine Information Center, 512 W. Maple Avenue, Suite 206, Vienna, VA 22180, (703) 938-DPT-3.

In the publication *East West,* an article by Richard Leviton "Who Calls the Shots?" Harris Coulter, Ph.D., and Barbara Fisher give statistics from their research regarding reactions and side effects of the DPT shot:

> [Coulter and Fisher] calculated that, based on the infant population of 3.3 million per year eligible for DPT shots, 4,248 children have either post-injection convulsions or collapse, 10,377 have high-pitched screaming within forty-eight hours, and 18,873 infants have some form of significant neurological reaction within two days. Possibly as many as 943 deaths and 11,666 cases of long-term damage are attributable to DPT.

Medical authorities from the A.M.A. (American Medical Association) as well as the A.A.P. (American Academy of Pediatrics) object, stating that the documentation Fisher and Coulter present (pulled from interviews with mothers of children affected by vaccines) is only anecdotal and cannot be scientifically admitted as substantiated research.[14]

This objection comes from a group that dismisses all nonmedical approaches and nonmedical criticisms as being unscientific, a group who in their own publication *(New England Journal of Medicine,* April 1995) claimed that the drugs they prescribe for their patients are tested using techniques that create the best possibility that the drugs will be found safe and effective.

This study found that in actual use, drug effectiveness and side effects differ substantially from those in initial clinical trials performed during the required FDA approval process.

A major reason for the variance is that drug researchers use ideal candidates on which to test their drugs. For example, patients with particular health problems or those who vary from the norm are excluded. Test subjects are therefore "ideal" and differ greatly from the typical patient of an average physician's practice.[15]

What the medical profession defines as scientific, it appears, is "anything we do and nothing that they do" the "they" being nonmedical interests.

Unfortunately, since medicine holds a virtual monopoly on accepted scientific conclusions, what medicine says usually goes. This also holds true in what the media choose to print or broadcast. For example, while Heather Whitestone was pursuing the title of Miss America in 1994, the press reported that her deafness (which made her an unusual candidate for the title) was due to the DPT vaccination (diphtheria, pertussis, and tetanus) which had been administered to her at approximately 18 months of age. She spoke freely about this during an interview with the *Birmingham News* as did her mother in an interview reported in *The Star* as well as with reporters from other broadcast and print media.

Once Whitestone won the title, medicine's public relations team wasted little time putting their spin on the story. In just a few days, headlines shouted a different interpretation. For example, *USA Today* printed the revised story on Monday, September 26, 1994, under the headline, "Miss America's Deafness Not Related to Vaccination," within days of her coronation.[16]

What was behind this news release? The reasons were obvious. How could the AAP (pediatrics academy) let the public think a vaccination did this to Miss America? Who'd want to have their own child receive a DPT shot after hearing the news that America's reigning queen was hurt by one? Medicine couldn't allow that to happen, so in a timely manner her doctor revealed that it wasn't the vaccination at all that caused Miss America's deafness, but an infection. For years no one thought anything other than DPT was the likely cause, but another culprit amazingly surfaces immediately after she wins the title.

To medicine's critics, this damage control effort demonstrated irresponsibility by medical professionals attempting to play down the known dangers of vaccinations. It was also irresponsible for someone as well known as a Miss America to be party to the giant that is medicine, especially when children are at risk. Finally, it was irresponsible for the media, including *USA Today*, to print the newfound medical allegation as gospel, as fact. Instead, they might have used the new report as a springboard for an investigative response, which might have begun with the headline, "Medical Authorities *Allege* Vaccination Did Not Cause Miss America's Deafness." Instead the headline, "Miss America's deafness not related to vaccination" ran without any questions or serious challenges posed by any journalist. This is one example of many in virtually all forms of popular media, where what medicine says "goes," whether that message is valid or not.

The vaccination movement is strong and growing stronger with each renewed effort on medicine's part. When there is another disease to attack, the public can be sure another vaccination offering will enter the arena. The newest fruit in the immunization cornucopia is the chickenpox vaccine. Its cost was estimated at approximately $40 per shot when introduced for general use in May of 1995.

Proponents of the new drug, including the Centers for Disease Control (CDC), say that chickenpox is basically an inescapable childhood illness. They claim that chickenpox carries direct and indirect costs of $384 million, including medical expenses and parents' lost wages. The illness strikes 3.7 million Americans each year with more than 90 percent of cases in children under 15. It kills approximately 100 children and results in 9,000 hospitalizations. R. Gordon Douglas, Jr., MD, president of the vaccine division of chickenpox vaccine manufacturer Merck & Co. says that, "[The new chickenpox vaccine] represents a milestone in the effort to prevent and eliminate common infectious disease through the use of vaccines."[17]

In direct contrast, other informed citizens who oppose wholesale use of the new drug look ten years into the future and see a nasty scenario unfolding. While the majority of children may be protected by a single dose of the chickenpox vaccine, immunity lasts only about 10 years. The chance that people will begin contracting chickenpox when they are older is of great concern. Chickenpox is a much more serious illness when contracted at age 40 than at age 4. Symptoms in children are usually mild and the average duration of the infection is three or four days. With adults, the disease can run one or two weeks and is far more likely to lead to complications such as shingles than when the disease is contracted by children, according to

Robert A. Bazell in *The New Republic* Article, "Spotty Records."

Bazell adds, "Most pharmaceutical companies can only fantasize about finding three and a half million new customers every year for one of their products," as he refers to the chickenpox vaccine.[18]

The same can be said for pediatricians, who will benefit by winning higher profits with this new vaccine.

Another concern is the fact that the vaccine is comprised of a live DNA-virus. Long-term repercussions of using DNA-comprised viruses in human beings cannot be predicted at this point. Finally, the cost benefits of using this vaccine in the United States are also debatable. *The Lancet* reports that the cost of chickenpox immunizations is expected to run at least $250 million dollars in the United States alone.[19]

Those opposed to immunizations believe that illnesses such as mumps, chicken pox, measles and others are a natural process of the body's immune system. When an illness is contracted, the immune system produces antibodies that help strengthen the body and provide overall physical defenses against disease throughout life. Compare this to immunizations which serve to bombard a young child's immune system with unnatural vaccines that lower physical defenses and may be responsible for a spectrum of autoimmune diseases in addition to side effects including damage to the brain and nervous system.

Vaccines constitute the most controversial element of medications for children, but others follow close behind. Two receiving much media attention are antibiotics and Ritalin.

In the early 1970s, a drug began to emerge from the shadows, one often prescribed for children labeled with minimal brain dysfunction (MBD) and its many behavioral symptoms including hyperactivity, hyperkinesis, learning disability, attention deficit disorder (ADD) and attention deficit hyperactivity disorder (ADHD), as well as those who were merely labeled "distracted". The reason behind the prescriptions was to make children more manageable, particularly in the classroom, and to help them learn.

Yet, from the beginning parents were concerned. Ritalin was a powerful drug that worked as an amphetamine-like cerebral stimulant. It was also habit-forming and came with a long list of potentially dangerous side effects. Even though the drug seemed a logical choice for severely affected hyperactive children, it was seen as a drastic measure for children with fewer problems. Parents, teachers and others became alarmed when doctors began prescribing the drug to an inordinate number of children.

In their 1979 book *The Tranquilizing of America*, published at a point of high controversy over the drug, Richard Hughes and Robert Brewin say,

> **The dispute [over the disorders Ritalin is prescribed for] centers not only on how [the disorders] are diagnosed and treated but also on [their] origin and, in fact, whether [these are real disorders] or a meaningless label to pin on children whose behavior is considered unacceptable by adults. The battle pits a small number of doctors and other health care professionals in alliance with an increasingly large and vocal number of parents against the most powerful institutions and industries in America— the federal government, organized medicine, the teaching profession, and the food, beverage, drug and chemical giants of the nation.**

Hughes and Brewin implicate food, drug and chemical companies because of the chemical additives they supply to the diets of Americans. These substances, including chemicals used to preserve product and enhance flavors, are a significant avenue of profit for big business. Dr. Ben Feingold, a pediatrician and allergist, discovered that by simply removing these additives from the diet, children's behavior often improves dramatically. The success rate following his program runs between 50 to 80 percent. This compares with the rate for behavioral improvement in children using drugs such as Ritalin, which is 60 to 80 percent.[20]

The preferred treatment should clearly be dietary, which is non-invasive and without side effects. However, drug therapy is often the physician's approach to unacceptable behavior in children. (Perhaps we should not be too harsh on doctors; rare is the medical school that focuses a fraction of its studies on nutrition compared to pharmaceuticals.) Once again, the drug, in this case Ritalin, is definitely a more profitable treatment mode. If children were to follow a corrective diet, pharmaceutical companies and food additive manufacturers alike would lose profits.

Concerned parent groups and other concerned citizens spurred a media blitz that hit a high in the mid to late 1980s. Ritalin use lost ground.

According to Daniel Safer and John Krager in a 1992 article that appeared in *The Journal of the American Medical Association*, the number of prescriptions fell for hyperactive and inattentive students because of well-publicized lawsuits over its use. Their stance was that the campaign against the use of Ritalin was not a wise one for the children.

The rate of medication with Ritalin for elementary and secondary students doubled every four to seven years from 1971 to 1987. After 20 lawsuits were filed throughout the United States and discussion was held on major national television shows and in print media, medication use dropped 39 percent for all students and 48 percent for elementary students.

The authors cited above concluded that 36 percent of children who were taken off medication realized some kind of school maladjustment . However, some parents whose children were already taking Ritalin were unaffected by the negative publicity because they were generally satisfied with the drug's effects on their children.

In a letter to the editor published in the May 12, 1993 issue of JAMA, Richard Vatz, Ph.D., responded to this assumption with a rebuttal, saying that Safer and Krager's article is flawed:

> **Safer and Krager's subtextual implications regarding the accuracy and consequences of the media coverage are insufficiently supported by their data. For example, the study concludes that 36 percent of the children taken off medication experienced "school maladjustment" but makes no effort to explain why 64 percent of the children taken off medication apparently experienced no**

major problems or whether the 36 percent claim of
problematic outcomes is adequately documented.

Vatz also questioned Safer and Krager's assumption
that parents of those children already on Ritalin were "satisfied" and were not affected by negative publicity. "Per-
ceptions of satisfaction, however, were not researched or
directly demonstrated and this conclusion represents another questionable implication regarding the prudence of
current drug therapy for children diagnosed as hyperactive," he said.

Vatz noted that attention deficit hyperactivity disorder
is a controversial medical problem and that Safer and
Krager have more "ambitious" reasons for writing the article. What Vatz means by the word "ambitious" is easy for
most close observers of the pharmaceutical industry to in-
terpret. In other words, Safer and Krager might serve a
financial angle in promoting Ritalin's use.[21]

We cannot leave the arena of inappropriate drug marketing for children without dealing with the subject of antibiotics, the most widely prescribed and abused drug category today.

Although few people, even critics of the way medicine
is practiced today, doubt the value of antibiotics in saving
lives, no one can dismiss the potential danger of antibiotics
to individuals and to our society in general. Parents bring
their children to family doctors and pediatricians for ailments such as colds and the flu. The same is true of adults
who refuse to let an illness run its course. These visits frequently result in a prescription for an antibiotic. This practice, medical researchers say, creates superinfections from
germs that have developed stronger survival traits after
encountering the antibiotics. Some of these supergerms have
already made their presence known, including the E.coli
bacteria that killed children in a fast-food restaurant and
strep-A, the unstoppable flesh-eating bacteria.

The late Robert S. Mendelsohn, MD author of *Confessions of a Medical Heretic,* wrote that doctors need to recognize that antibiotics must hold a severely limited place
in medicine. He notes that a typical person will need peni-

cillin only a handful of times during his or her entire life if it is prescribed only when the stakes are worth the risks.

The risks Mendelsohn refers to are superinfections, both on the individual and larger scale.

He writes:

> When an antibiotic fights one infection, it may encourage an even worse infection by a strain of bacteria that is resistant to the drug. Bacteria are remarkably adaptable organisms. Subsequent generations can develop resistance to a drug as their ancestors are exposed more and more. [22]

Stuart Levy, MD of Tufts University and author of *The Antibiotic Paradox* writes that when a person takes antibiotics, the medicine constantly bombards the weaker bacteria and selects the stronger ones to survive. In other words, the same antibiotics designed to kill bacteria and fight infection are actually creating supergerms that will be more resistant to antibiotics. To counter this process, new and more powerful antibiotics are constantly being developed. These stronger drugs, in turn, create even more resistant superbacteria than before. The fear is that someday a bacteria will develop that no drug will be able to stop.[23]

Another drawback of excessive use of antibiotics for children is that the drugs kill beneficial as well as harmful bacteria. By constantly taking antibiotics, children become highly susceptible to secondary infections because the helpful bacteria are not present to fight them. In addition, if a time should come when an individual needs an antibiotic to save his or her life, the person's body may have become resistant to antibiotics. Because a person takes antibiotics for a simple sore throat, an infection that has entered his body due to blood poisoning, for example, might be untreatable due to the body's acquired resistance to antibiotic therapy.

The dangers of antibiotics come in other forms beside direct medication. Antibiotics are present to an alarming degree in the meat and milk children and adults ingest. According to Stephen Sundlof, D.V.M., Ph.D., and head of the FDA's Center for Veterinary Medicine, livestock are routinely administered antibiotics to fight infection, and chickens are given drugs to stimulate growth. Milk, he notes, may legally contain trace amounts of eighty separate antibiotics. This kind of antibiotic ingestion contributes to the breeding of antibiotic resistant bacteria in both animals and people.[24]

A justifiable criticism can be raised that the medical industry, particularly the pharmaceutical sector, has reaped unprecedented profits, concerned more with the bottom line of their financial statements than the welfare of the public. An invasive approach to treating disease is the pharmaceutical companies' answer to healthcare. As a result, children as well as adults are subjected to more shots, more drugs, and more medical care. Besides profit there is no other logical reason why the pharmaceutical industry counters every negative attack on one of their products with an astute fact-dodging public relations effort rather than demonstrating proof of safety or efficacy.

In the medical marketplace, no possibility of pharmaceutical treatment is left unexplored. If there is a human condition where a drug might fit, there will be a fit, even if that human condition is not a true disease. Drug researchers have thought of a treatment for every condition that exists today. And, in the future, we can be sure, researchers will find even more conditions over which we must worry and seek drugs to "cure" these "conditions."

This strategy constitutes the drugging of America and plays out the saying that the treatment is worse than the cure. As for the youngest of our generations, the children, who have been given more medicine, administered more invasive treatment, and thereby been subjected to more compounds whose effects may not be known for years to come, more than any previous generation—for our children we have the most to fear.

1. Schedule of Standard Procedures, Pediatrics, P.C., Kalamazoo, MI (pediatrics office), Revised 11/94.

2. *The American Chiropractor,* Tedd Koren, D.C., (columnist), March/April 1995, pg. 38.

3. "Vaccine Information: A Guide for Parents," National Vaccine Information Center (NVIC), 512 Maple Rd., #206, Vienna, V 22180, (703) 938-DPT3, 1994, pg.7.

4. *Medical Nemesis,* Ivan Illich, Pantheon Books, New York, 1976, pgs. 15-16.

5. *Vaccines: Are They Really Safe and Effective?,* Neil Z. Miller, New Atlantean Press, Santa Fe, New Mexico, 1994, pgs. 18-46.

6. Illich, pgs. 16-17.

7. Miller, pgs 18-45.

8. *Vaccination: The Medical Assault on the Immune System*, Viera Schiebner, Ph.D., 1993.

9. *Vaccination, Social Violence and Criminality*, Center for Empirical Medicine, Harris Coulter, Ph.D., 1990.

10. "They Had No Voice...They Had No Choice," (brochure), National Vaccine Information Center, Vienna, VA.

11. "They Had No Voice...They Had No Choice," (brochure), NVIC, Vienna, VA.

12. "Vaccine Information: A Guide For Parents," pgs 7-9, NVIC, Vienna, VA, 1994.

13. *The Vaccine Reaction*, Vol 1, No. 1, March 1995, NVIC, Vienna, VA.

14. *East West,* Richard Leviton, November 1988.

15. *New England Journal of Medicine*, April 28, 1995.

16. "Miss America's Deafness Not Related To Vaccination," *USA Today*, September 26, 1994, pg 4D.

17. "Chickenpox Vaccine Promises Protection, Cost Savings," Deborah L. Shelton, *American Medical News*, April 3, 1995, v38 n13 p5(1).

18. "Spotty Record," Robert Bazell, *The New Republic,* January 20, 1992, v205, n30, p16 (2).

19. "Controversy about Chickenpox," (editorial) *The Lancet,* September 12, 1992, v340, n8820, p639 (2).

20. *The Tranquilizing of America (Pill Popping and the American Way of Life),* Richard Hughes and Robert Brewin, Harcourt Brace Jovanovich, New York, 1979, pp 114-116.

21. Letter to the Editor, Richard Vatz, Ph.D., et al, (in the May 12, 1993 issue of the *Journal of the American Medical Association. (JAMA).*

22. *Confessions of a Medical Heretic,* Robert S. Mendelsohn, MD, Warner Books, New York, 1979, pg 55.

23. *The Antibiotic Paradox,* Stuart Levy, MD, Plenum Books, 1992.

24. "Defend Yourself Against Supergerms," Jack Challem, *Natural Health*, March/April 1995, pgs 56-57.

9

Medicine's Evolution to Pharmacy

Medicine's development dates back to the beginning of man's existence when cures—however crude— were sought for the ills of the time. It wasn't until the Middle Ages (AD 500-1500) that medicine began to organize and set out on its long evolution to twentieth century health care.

In the Middle Ages, specialists were trained through apprenticeships to become midwives, herb gatherers, compounders, bonesetters, hernia specialists, cataract couchers, stonecutters (lithotomists who made incisions of the bladder to remove stones) and barber-surgeons. Yet, outside of loosely structured guilds that established training and fees during this era, the practice of medicine was basically unregulated. Medicine with all its facets was considered a trade, not a profession.

Yet, even from the beginning, there existed a movement to regulate and improve the standards of those who practiced medicine. The goal of this movement was to produce doctors who were highly educated, research-trained and clinically experienced, a far cry from the bloodletters who were more proficient in cutting hair, their other specialty.

Between 1650 and 1850, medicine made massive strides in that transition to professionalism and respectability. While the United States was somewhat slower in its development than countries in Europe because it was also struggling to become a nation, by 1850 this country was also well on its way to defining professional protocol.

The campaign to organize and regulate medical practices in the United States was a much needed effort. Without guidelines, a doctor's qualifications could range from being trained in a prestigious European medical school to practicing with little or no training at all. The effort to regulate succeeded in producing a more competent field of physicians. At the same time a secondary reaction to the organizing and regulating of medicine ushered in a less altruistic outcome, a capitalistic one.

In his book, *Encyclopedia of Medical History,* Roderick E. McGrew writes:

> **Economic factors also favored reform. The nineteenth-century proliferation of schools and students flooded and depressed the market for medical services, and both doctors and medical students had a poor public image...Introducing curricular reforms based on scientific medicine could be expected to drive all but the most firmly grounded medical schools to the wall, while enhanced standards for admission and performance could only reduce the number of practitioners. In a numerically smaller profession, the public image could improve as higher standards were expected to attract a "better" sort of person and the social status of the profession would rise. All of this would substantially increase the economic value of a medical degree.**

The 1909 appointment of Abraham Flexner by the Carnegie Foundation for the Advancement of Teaching moved reform along quickly. After an examination of medical schools, the Flexner Report touted a need for doctors to have an education in the liberal arts, basic science, scientific instruction, clinical training, research and an internship, using John Hopkins Medical School as the ideal. Public and private support grew in response to Flexner's ideas and with it a shift in financial backing to those schools that met the standards Flexner had outlined. An avalanche of efforts to comply followed and in its wake, only a fraction of the previously existing medical schools met the standards Flexner had outlined.

McGrew notes that, "By 1928, only 74 regular medical schools remained out of the 154 counted two decades earlier, and this number declined further in the next five years."

The subsequent drop in ratio between doctor and patient followed and medicine began its climb into elitism and increased financial gain.[1]

According to James P. Carter, MD, the Flexner Report had a widespread effect on medicine beyond the issue of which medical schools would continue to exist and even beyond who would become doctors and become financially successful. The report allowed the corporate world to cash in as well. Carter asserts that the report caught the attention and incited the ingenuity of many including someone by the name of Rockefeller.

The Flexner guidelines were accepted in theory and later in application by John D. Rockefeller who through the Rockefeller Foundation found a way to tie these guidelines to his oil holdings. Rockefeller realized that if he could help expedite medical education, he could simultaneously increase his own financial gain by contributing to research projects that would be conducted at selected medical schools, research that involved his business interests.

Rockefeller's objectives as developed through his foundation included the following:

1. To preserve family fortune from inheritance and taxation

2. To use education to change society and mold the public's views

3. To use foundation money under the cloak of
public good in order to fund commercial and
ideological ventures with tax-exempt dollars, all
under the name of philanthropy.

Rockefeller realized, according to Carter:

Because of the importance of the biological
sciences and of the scientific method [the research
principle Flexner advocated that he believed to be
a necessary element of medical education] the
major drug companies at the time (spearheaded by
the move of Standard Oil of New Jersey into the
development and manufacture of oil-based,
synthetic drugs) were able to exert a great deal of
influence on the medical schools by supporting
research in pharmacology and by supporting
clinical drug trials...The drug trials constituted a
significant portion of the research conducted by
medical schools. To many physicians, [drugs and
drug trials] became synonymous with science in
medicine.

The Flexner Report provided the ammunition medicine
needed to organize and regulate itself. Yet, while standards
of the medical profession urgently needed upgrading at the
time, the report also set in motion certain elements that at
first appeared to be altruistic yet turned out to be based on
highly self-serving goals. The drug industry discovered in
this report the opportunity it needed to tie itself and its
synthetic drug products to medicine. The Flexner Report
said "research" needed to be a part of all medical school
training. Foundations like the Rockefeller Foundation
jumped at the chance to make "research" synonymous with
"drug development," although research could realistically
involve many other kinds of studies as well.

Students of Rockefeller's role in the courtship and marriage of the pharmaceutical and medical professions may
be kinder to the great industrialist and philanthropist than
he deserves. Most depict him as a facilitator of modern
medicine rather than examining his professional interests
in its developing and highly discriminatory form.

Another effect of the regulation movement ensured the
monopoly medicine holds until today. As synthetic drugs

and medicine became inseparable partners, other avenues of care such as homeopathy, manipulative medicine and herbal medicine lost their ranking as accepted methods of health care.[2]

Because medicine now embraced the use and development of drugs, various branches of healthcare that had previously been thought of as a part of the medical profession were quickly considered substandard. Non-drug healthcare fell into the realm of what medicine would now label "charlatans" and "quacks" because their methods were not "scientific," according to the new medicine.

From that point on, the evolution of medical training and drug development moved forward in parallel. One could not exist without the other. The Rockefeller Foundation's gifts to medical schools and scientific research set the precedent that is still followed today, the marriage of medicine and drugs coexisting in a long and profitable union.

Even so, that marriage would not be controversial if drugs were inherently safe and effective or if drugs were the key to good health. This is not the case. Drugs are toxic by nature, and their toxicity often causes much more harm than good. As Andrew Weil notes, drugs are inherently dangerous—the only difference between a drug and a poison is dosage.[3]

Drugs, however, were not always synthetic chemicals and because of this, they were infinitely less toxic in their virgin state. Early medicines date back to ancient times when natural substances were used to relieve and control illness. Roderick McGrew points out that "[Today's] pharmacy is a modern profession with an ancient tradition..," that ancient tradition dating back to the oldest existing records from the third millennium B.C. where artifacts reveal a "fully developed tradition in which natural products [were] used for specific medical purposes." These ancient drugs were made of vegetables, minerals and other substances including alcohol, fats and oils, animal parts, milk, honey and wax.[4]

Natural compounds, including herbs, were the primary ingredients of therapeutic drugs up until the early 1800s when scientists first began isolating and refining pure ingredients from plants. The first to be isolated was narcotine and morphine from opium.[5]

Isolating pure ingredients meant that a drug could now be given in an exact dosage whereas in plant or in other natural form, that dosage level was not measurable. Isolating drugs also meant that the patient experienced a greater level of risk that the drug would be toxic. According to Weil:

> In general, isolated and refined drugs are much more toxic than their botanical sources. [Isolated drugs] also tend to produce effects of more rapid onset, greater intensity, and shorter duration. Sometimes they fail to reproduce desirable actions of plants they come from, and sometimes they lack natural safeguards present in those plants. They also lend themselves to methods of administration favoring abuse and toxicity.

Weil also points out that medicine itself has an erroneous belief that "plants and isolated active principles [drugs] are equivalent."

The foxglove plant is an example of a natural substance having built-in safeguards. Used for correcting irregular heartbeat, it became refined for use as a drug called digitalis. However, when foxglove itself is used to correct heartbeat irregularities and too much of the plant is administered, the patient will experience stomach problems which might include nausea and stomach aches. The dosage would then be cut back. When synthesized foxglove is administered in the form of digitalis, an overdose will not create digestive problems, but arrhythmia, or irregular heartbeat, ultimately a more serious condition.

Weil explains:

> Whatever the compounds are in foxglove that irritate the stomach, they are not [the same compounds as those found in digitalis]. They are not the heart-stimulating compounds at all but, rather, associate compounds that occur along with them... In other words, the whole plant has certain built-in safety mechanisms that are lost when its [other elements] are refined out and used in pure form. Call this the wisdom of nature.[6]

Today natural therapeutic substances are predominantly relegated to health food stores and to practitioners of holistic health. Their use among mainstream medicine is minimal; synthetic chemical drugs constitute the majority of doctor-prescribed treatments, and because pharmaceutical interests hold the corner on the drug market, natural substances used throughout history up to this century are now scorned by the medical profession. Of the thousands of natural substances, from vitamins and minerals, to herbs and others, organized medicine has little positive to say about them and in fact, has moved to diminish their use, outlaw them and slander those practitioners who use them. Ironically, efforts have even been made to regulate these products so only medical doctors would be able to prescribe their use.

This question comes to mind: "Why does medicine seek to control products that they neither understand nor condone? Why does medicine wish to control something they know nothing about but can only criticize?" The answer is simple: It is the easiest way to minimize their use.

Only recently has medicine acknowledged any therapeutic use of vitamins and minerals. The few applications generally acknowledged include folic acid to help prevent birth defects and a handful of others. Yet, natural healthcare practitioners and aficionados have touted hundreds of these natural remedies for decades, while a large share of these substances have been advocated for centuries by cultures including the Chinese, Indians, Egyptians and ancient Greeks.

Today, medicine doesn't have the final word when it comes to healthcare choices. When medicine doesn't work, when it fails to prevent illness or fails to treat it successfully when illness occurs, people are migrating in increasing numbers to alternative care. One in three people now seeks some form of alternative care. People are buying vitamins and other supplements, consulting with chiropractors, naturopaths, homeopaths and others because orthodox medicine has failed them in the treatment of most chronic and debilitating illnesses including cancer, diabetes and heart disease. Medicine can only treat these illnesses with a steady stream of highly powerful, often toxic drugs. Alternative medicine offers hope for wellness without drugs.

The lion's share of the bill for alternative care (services and products) is paid for by the patient. Since medicine doesn't condone it, insurance won't cover it. A Boston pain specialist who believes preventive care is not given a chance to prove itself says, "Society actually discourages preventive medicine because the insurance companies don't pay for it. Instead, insurance encourages treatment and testing once the disease process occurs. . ." The specialist uses the example of medicine offering codeine for pain (a powerful, addictive drug) when a safer method would be a series of therapeutic treatments.[7]

Medicine's scorn of natural remedies and the denial of payment by insurance companies for their use is seen by some as a breach of antitrust law. Medicine maintains a monopoly of the healthcare market while the government looks the other way. Not only does the government look the other way regarding medicine's unlawful monopoly, but the United States government also gives its complete approval and overt support and cooperation to medicine through its policing arm: the FDA.

When there is no true competition, there is little incentive for improved care, for better products or services. There is only incentive for profit. The existing system profits by treating the sick and dying, not by keeping the patient well. There is more money in establishing a regimen of pills and surgery for the sick and dying than in prescribing preventive care for the healthy. The report issued by Abraham Flexner in the early 1900s, allowed medicine to set its course for monopoly ruled by greed.

There it remains.

Medical doctors who realize there must be a better way to treat illness and attempt to practice with procedures that are not approved by the medical establishment (non-drug, nonsurgical therapies) are usually ostracized, threatened, and frequently have their licenses threatened by their own governing boards for using "unscientific" or "unsound" treatments. The medical monopoly calls its own shots, having no one else to answer to since the FDA and government policy in general allow the monopoly to thrive. Supported by the government, medicine determines what will and what will not be categorized as scientifically sound, and excludes all other avenues that cannot meet its narrow parameters. "Scientifically sound" can be interpreted as anything that has not been tested and approved through FDA mandated methodology. That approval process allegedly attests to the safety and efficacy of a product. It takes several years and often hundreds of millions in dollars to obtain approval, a price only the most wealthy pharmaceutical companies can afford. To test the safety and effectiveness of vitamins, of minerals, herbs, organic glandulars and other commonly used natural substances is out of reach for most business interests. Cost is not the only factor. No one company can hold the patent on a natural substance—Vitamin C, for example—even if the firm has funded extensive research on its benefits and appropriate use in treating and preventing illness. On the other hand, once a synthetic drug has been developed, approved and patented, the drug company has several years to maintain a monopoly on its use. Consequently, medicine holds the market captive on the label "scientific" and on products approved by the establishment.

The general public has been conditioned by propaganda to the degree that most people believe that drugs can make them well. The fact remains that while drugs are designed to control conditions to varying degrees— lower bad cholesterol, reduce blood pressure, regulate sugar levels, etc.—these drugs will not return the body to health. The control the drug provides is artificial; if the patient stops taking the drug, the condition will likely return. Because drugs do not return the body to health and are only artificial controls (the body is not using its own powers) that stop once the drug is no longer taken, they are often prescribed for the long-term, frequently creating lifelong dependence.

In addition, patients may take several drugs simultaneously. In combination, these drugs produce even more side effects—all without strengthening the body.

Long-term, lifelong dependence on the medical system for constant care in chronic illness provides lifelong revenue for medical interests. In most cases the cost of medication and care far exceeds its benefits.

The negative evolution of medical history has brought healthcare in the United States to a monopolistic system of ineffective and cost prohibitive care for chronic and degenerative illness. The fault appears to lie in an evolutionary process that increasingly has grown nepotistic and profit mongering. Together these elements have created a healthcare system that in the late twentieth century is as sickly as the people for which it cares. Much of the fault for this can be directly linked to the development of the pharmaceutical industry with its ingenious blending into the system of health delivery, so that the two have become one and the same.

To ensure success, this union is brought to the government through its powerful lobbying groups whose goal is to sway elected officials to establish law and policy that will be conducive to their interests. Additionally, through its ties to the media, medicine encourages editorial policies that work in its favor. It is here that the deal is sealed—bringing the words of big business to the public, the words taken as gospel to the people who open their wallets.

A prime example of this inbred system is evidenced in a 1992 article printed in the publication *New Statesman & Society* entitled, "Consider the Lilly" by Alexander Cockburn. In his treatise, Cockburn states that the close kinship the Eli Lilly company enjoyed with the Bush-Quayle administration brought the pharmaceutical giant favors that were assisted by the major media, particularly in Lilly's battle with the Church of Scientology. The subject: Drug Policy and Prozac. The players: Eli Lilly, the government, the American press.

The scenario:

Prologue: Eli Lilly's first Washington lobby was organized by Dan Quayle's uncle, in 1959. The Indiana-based company and its connection to the Quayle family is inescapable.

Act I, Scene 1: George Bush, after leaving the CIA and before running for the 1980 Republican nomination and subsequently becoming President of the United States, works for Eli Lilly. He later removes the directorship position he held with Lilly from his resume' but continues unofficial lobbying for the company as Vice President. Bush also fails to disclose his ownership of Lilly Stock.

Scene 2: Following the 1988 presidential campaign victory, George Bush assigns Vice President Dan Quayle to head the Council on Competitiveness (which Cockburn says was responsible for "taking calls from corporate chieftains and jumping to their commands"). Through the council, Lilly is asked to review the FDA's approval procedures. Soon after, the FDA lengthens the time a pharmaceutical company can maintain its product exclusivity (which extended patent protection to 17 years from the original patent date), meaning a drug company could now reap even more profits before competitors can bring a generic version of a drug to the market.

Scene 3: As Lilly's vice president for corporate affairs overseeing government lobbying, Mitch Daniels had worked with the Reagan/Bush administration. In November 1991, Daniels co-chairs a fund-raiser that brings in $600,000 for the Bush/Quayle campaign.

Scene 4: Bush and Quayle flag biotech products as needing faster approval by the FDA. Eli Lilly's commitment to biotech products was already a fact with its strategy of buying rights to other companies' drugs, offering research capital and marketing power.

Scene 5: In order to corner the health products market, Bush/Quayle's FDA begins campaigning to ban sales of 400 plus over-the-counter products ranging from holistic nostrums (vitamins/minerals, etc.) to aspirin and codeine, Cockburn notes. The goal—*every* pill, *every* medicine would be sold under a brand name or issued by prescription. "Control" and "monopoly" were the goals.

Scene 6: The FDA allows that the testing and approval process of drugs can be done by outside scientists (a loosely defined term primarily meaning non-governmental). As Ralph Nader's Public Citizens' Congress Watch put it: "Not only do outside reviewers lack the training necessary to conduct thorough safety reviews, but...most non-governmental scientists receive funding from the same drug companies seeking approval for new products." (An example of continued conflict of interest.)

Scene 7: Enter Prozac, worth $760 million in sales in 1990. Reports of Prozac's side effects come to the surface. Lawsuits are filed. Eli Lilly hesitatingly warns doctors about the problems with Prozac. The Church of Scientology's Commission on Human Rights urges Congress to ban Prozac from the market. (Between June and August, Eli Lilly's stock drops by 20 percent, a $5.8 billion decrease in overall value.)

Scene 8: The Climax (eight months later) The *Wall Street Journal* publishes a scathing attack on the Church of Scientology and its founder L. Ron Hubbard. The story greatly pleases Eli Lilly and its public relations firm Burson Marsteller. Next, *Time* magazine follows WSJ's lead and prints an expose' on the church that Cockburn says, was full of factual errors including one on the church's income— $503 million instead of the actual $4 million. Lilly buys a quarter of a million copies of the edition and distributes them to doctors throughout the country, later offering doctors "indemnification against lawsuits if they would continue to prescribe Prozac."

Scene 9: The FDA pulls together an advisory committee to study the drug. Cockburn notes that five of the eight members have serious conflicts of interest, including those receiving financial backing from Lilly. The outcome of the committee is positive to Prozac continuing on the market.

Scene 10: The Church of Scientology makes points about the campaign engineered against its credibility, noting that the media itself has ties to Eli Lilly, i.e., Richard Wood, Eli Lilly's Chairman of the Board, president and CEO, serves on the board of Dow Jones (parent company of the *Wall Street Journal*). Nicholas J. Nicholas, recent past CEO of Time Warner, parent company of *Time*, has a brother Peter M. Nicholas, a senior executive at Eli Lilly who coincidentally is married to Ruth Virginia Lilly.

Scene 11: In order to gain even further clout for the piece, *Time* itself soon nominates the writer of the anti-Scientology *Time* article, Richard Behar, for journalistic prizes. He receives the Conscience of Media Award from the American Society of Journalists and Authors as well as the Worth Bingham prize awarded for public interest journalism. Behar also receives the Gerald Loeb Award for Distinguished Business and Financial Journalism. The connection of the last award: J. Clayburn LaForce has served simultaneously as chairman of the Loeb foundation as well as a director for Eli Lilly.[8]

Denouement (Resolution): Prozac continues as one of the top ten best selling drugs in the United States.

Finally, an example of the incest between corporations and government appeared in columnist Molly Ivins's July 1995 column, "Deregulatin' Fools Eye Targets." It points to the issue of deregulating "toxic chemicals, dangerous drugs and rotten food, for starters." Ivins calls the Republicans "deregulatin fools," but her point is not entirely made in jest.

When our policy and lawmakers want to repeal or prevent legislation that would help ensure the public safety from being enacted, the public is in trouble. When that group of lawmakers wants to repeal past legislation such as The Delaney Clause, which forbids the slightest trace of carcinogens in our foods, how can they be trusted with the health and welfare of their constituents? Ivins poses this, "Why, you may ask, would anyone be opposed to regulations that clearly save lives?" She answers the question with an Upton Sinclair quote: "It is difficult to get a man to understand something when his salary depends on his not understanding it."

The lobbyists instead of the American people are winning their battles in Washington, but this is not what former Senate Majority Leader Bob Dole would like the public to believe. Dole wants us to believe that regulation is always bad for the public. "It is clear that the American people are fed up with a regulatory state that is out of control," he says. Mr. Dole must be patronizing a public that he believes is either brain dead or who feels utterly helpless.

Maybe we are both—brain dead and helpless—but primarily we are confused.

According to Ivins, the deregulating measures have been spread around in several different bills so that even those who are alert and might not feel so helpless, probably won't see what is coming "down the pike."[9] The lawyers know how to work it. Their skill is in "words" and "strategy" and those who lead our country are very good at both tools. They can tell us "I'm doing it for my constituents" when they really mean, "It's important my constituents think I'm doing it for them."

In the arena of healthcare, what appears on the surface, on the lips of our doctors, our government and our media is diatribe disguised in a never-ending torrent of feigned altruism directed toward the masses. Still, most people know the score. Even Dole's "brain-dead" public recognizes that few efforts in the name of health care are ultimately made for them. The efforts are directed at one purpose: the financial gain of big business and in this case, that business is the very big business of chemistry.

1. *Encyclopedia of Medical History,* Roderick E. McGrew, McGraw-Hill, 1985, pp. 179-183.

2. *Racketeering in Medicine, The Suppression of Alternatives,* James P. Carter, MD, Dr. P.H., Hampton Roads Publishing Co., Inc. 1993, pgs. xxiv-xxviii.

3. *Health and Healing,* Andrew Weil, Houghton Mifflin, 1988, pg 96.

4. *Encyclopedia of Medical History*, Roderick McGrew, pg. 250-251.

5. *Encyclopedia of Medical History*, McGrew, p 256.

6. *Health and Healing*, Weil, pp. 99, 104

7. *A Different Kind of Healing,* Oscar Janiger, MD and Philip Goldberg, Tarcher/Putnam, 1994, pp 189.

8. *New Statesman & Society*, Alexander Cockburn, Nov 27, 1992, v5, n230, p26 (1).

9. "Deregulatin' Fools Eye Targets," Molly Ivins, *Fort Worth Star-Telegram*, July, 1995.

10

A New Kind of Healing: People Before Profit

Medical doctors repeat the Hippocratic Oath as they become health care professionals, as they become "doctors of healing." In part, that pledge swears them to keep their patients from harm and to give no deadly drugs. Yet drugs are inherently toxic and because drugs are toxic, they are often harmful and known to be deadly as well. So what kind of physician is it who prescribes for his patients drugs whose effects are virtually unknown? As the final paragraph of the oath reads:

> If I fulfill this oath and do not violate it, may it be granted to me to enjoy life and art, being honored with fame among all men for all time to come; if I transgress it and swear falsely, may the opposite of all this be my lot.

What kind of physician is it who swears one set of goals, yet pursues another? Perhaps it's simply that doctors are trained to be ignorant of the true dangers of drugs or that drugs serve as the physician's primary choice of treatment because practitioners have been inadequately trained in non-drug protocol. When medications are in play, the potential for harm is strong. Should the physician then ignore the oath?

The essence of the creed, the oath, rings with an intrinsic flaw: "To do no harm, to come for the benefit of the sick." Instead it would be more convincing if it were to read, "To be of help (rather than "to do no harm"), and to benefit the healthy (not only "the sick"). Why should the doctor wait for the patient to attain illness before something is done? Why shouldn't doctors assume that health itself needs to be maintained, that health needs close attention and care? Why is illness medicine's priority?

Patients with early signs of health problems are often told by medical doctors to wait to see if the condition worsens. Until the patient's state of health reaches a point at which invasive care is necessary, medicine has few answers in its drug- and surgery-based system. By that time the optimal point to catch a problem has passed, yet that is the point at which medicine most frequently enters the picture, the point at which care that is both expensive and of questionable worth is initiated.

In his book, *Health and Healing*, Andrew Weil suggests that medicine lacks "any clear concept of health," and the absence of this concept leads its practitioners to pay more attention to disease. He adds, "I heard the word *health* mentioned very infrequently during four years of medical school...allopathic doctors give lip service to preventive medicine..."[1]

This point is the major criticism of medical care today: medicine and all its related industries function optimally with disease rather than with health. Opponents of medicine as it is practiced today say that the existing system of health care in the United States rewards the sick by paying for disease care, but punishes the healthy. Those who try to remain healthy by using methods of preventive care

are responsible for underwriting the costs of their own health maintenance.

Yet preventive care is less expensive: educating people to eat more healthfully, exercise regularly, take vitamins to supplement inadequacies in the diet, and bolster the immune system through any number of nontraditional therapies—all in order to prevent the primary killer diseases of our time: cancer, diabetes, and heart disease. These therapies, including homeopathy, acupuncture, chiropractic and others, focus on allowing the body to use its own powers of healing, rather than merely attempting to control disease through artificial means as medicine attempts to do. Nonmedical therapies are a much less expensive proposition compared with the hundreds of thousands of dollars spent once a person needs heart surgery, cancer therapy or years of drugs and intensive treatment. Yet these nonmedical approaches are the very therapies that medicine shuns and criticizes as being unscientific and practiced by mere quacks.

Even so, it would appear profit-smart for insurance companies to reward wellness—even to launch a concerted effort with full participation of its insured clients to attempt wellness— rather than wait until illness comes into play and then pay the cost of expensive disease care. At first, the answer seems to be "yes"; there is money in trying to keep people healthy instead of only paying for heart surgery, cancer therapy, and a steady stream of prescription drugs. However, on closer inspection, illness care makes more sense—dollars and cents— because there is ultimately far more profit in illness than in health even for the insurance industry.

To understand this, we need to look at the gambling principle. People don't take out insurance and pay hundreds of dollars a month betting that they'll stay well. People take out insurance and pay hundreds of dollars a month betting that someday they will attain a state of illness. If, instead, people were to bet that they will remain healthy— that they would require few benefits during their lifetime— chances are that they would take out less health insurance. This would not settle well with insurance company profits.

A parallel example is auto insurance. If an auto owner believed he'd never have an accident, he would likely take out a minimum of insurance, only that required by law. Yet most people believe they will have an accident sooner or later—at least make a claim against their insurance due to one incident or another— because most drivers realize that either they themselves are unsafe drivers or the people they meet on the road will be. This is why auto insurance is important. People believe they will someday get sick just as they believe someday they will have an auto insurance claim. Pay hundreds now to save thousands later. We bet on illness, just as we bet on having accidents. Betting on auto accidents, just as betting on disease, ultimately means more insurance policies, with higher premiums, and ultimately more profit for the insurance industry.

The public bets on illness because chances are, in a person's lifetime, he will—

Eat foods that are full of additives and processed, with much of the nutritional value processed out

Live in a toxic environment, where chemicals compromise health quality

Not exercise regularly take in further toxic substances including soft drinks, alcohol, licit and illicit drugs and other chemicals in food.

How can this average person expect to remain healthy?

Insurance companies bank on unhealthy lifestyles, on a public desperate to be insured because of the probability that most will experience serious illness during their lifetime. Few people can pay for the healthcare medicine deems necessary once disease enters the picture. The tests, the drugs, the surgeries—all are cost prohibitive to a single individual or a family. Only the insurance companies can be counted on to foot the bill for those who do experience serious illness.

On the other hand, there are those with lifestyles that lead to good health and who believe there are lifelong benefits associated with preventive care. Although being insured is still important because health is an unknown entity, this category of people will likely use fewer prescription drugs, visit their doctors less and require fewer medical procedures. Lifestyles that lead to health develop healthier people who need less medical care and fewer drugs. Chances are, this "healthier" individual will feel comfortable spending less money for insurance that provides benefits for drugs and doctor visits. The "healthier" citizen probably wants only catastrophic insurance, especially when an increasing share of the insurance premium is coming out of pocket. Without a continual need for doctors and drugs, this kind of individual could pay much lower premiums, and insurance company income would be dramatically reduced.

The fear of illness and the bet that illness will enter the picture (that wager being paid for with insurance premiums) keeps the public paying and the insurance industry financially strong. This is one more way the corporation wins—by keeping its public unhealthy and by not encouraging its good health.

Yet even with this grim picture, the face of our nation's health care shows signs of change. Part of this change involves dissent in the ranks of the medical profession, many of whom have become disillusioned. The profit-centered interest of the industry as a whole does not settle well with a growing number of health care professionals who sees the contradiction between health and medicine and are dismayed that medicine's focus is not necessarily health oriented.

These practitioners are questioning their profession's value as well as its ethics in the care of chronic and degenerative illness. In increasing numbers, they are asking: "What is our profession's goal? The patient or the profit?" The fact that "obscene profit" seems to be an inseparable piece of the medical pie has brought many practitioners to reevaluate their work, allowing them to see that they, in fact, have turned into the ultimate salespeople, serving up the expensive drugs and treatment for an industry obsessed with "big bucks."

This growing faction of medical professionals has become disillusioned not only with their profession's focus on the treatment of disease rather than the promotion of

health, but with all the related industries—insurance, prescription drugs, surgery and invasive care. They realize that
this powerful commercial complex treats chronic and degenerative disease with methods that most often result in
failure. They understand that failing to keep people healthy
results in profit for the medical profession and vast profits
for the pharmaceutical industry.

For too long only a few have questioned medicine's failure to conquer illness.

Gary Null, who has testified on health issues before
the U.S. Congress, says in his book, *Healing Your Body
Naturally*:

> **Ironically, in our society, we do not look at the
> failures of traditional medicine. We do not look at
> the fact that upwards of 75 percent of all coronary
> bypass operations have been shown to be
> ineffective and should not have been performed.
> We do not look at the 500,000 Americans dying of
> cancer each year, many of whom had the best and
> brightest physicians within the orthodox
> community administering the accepted [medical]
> treatments: chemotherapy, radiation, and surgery.
> We do not look at the millions of Americans who
> have been used as guinea pigs for new and
> frequently deadly drugs...Indeed, the real
> quackery, the real pseudo science...the desperation
> treatments that generally end in painful failure
> are most often found in the realm of orthodoxy
> [medicine].**

Null's book provides a perspective on the ways that the
politics and economics of traditional medicine work in excluding therapies not accepted by orthodox medicine in order to maintain the monopoly.[2]

In the end, everything is linked by the profit motive—
the media, the health care profession, the food industry,
the chemical industry, the insurance industry, all industries, one affecting the next in a never ending quest to produce larger and more astounding profit margins. But at
whose expense?

We could have a better car, a more fuel efficient car.
The technology is there. The knowhow exists. But how much

less would the oil, chemical and related industries make with a fuel-efficient car?

We could have a corporate America where more people were employed and making a better wage, enjoying a better standard of living, but how much less would the heads of companies make?

We could have a more accountable and efficient system of government, one that works for the interests of the people, but then how could the corporations and the cartels make as much money with an honest government?

Corporate lobbyists promote inefficient programs, systems treating the sick and not the healthy. What is best for the people is not what is best for the corporation, the politician or the person who grows wealthier from the profit-manipulated standards of services and products delivered to the American public.

Julian Whitaker, MD, in his book Guide to Natural Healing, poses the question:

> **Is it possible that the [medical healthcare] system is impure, that it actively works against the dissemination of useful and helpful information that cannot be classified as a patented prescription drug or expensive medical technology?**

Whitaker cites a U.S. Office of Technology statistic that 80 percent of conventional medical treatments have no basis in science, meaning that adequate studies have not been conducted that prove the effectiveness of a majority of medical treatments and that these are performed because of their popularity rather than their scientific basis.

These ineffective modalities include surgeries that have not been adequately researched, but are conducted because they have simply become accepted by the medical community. (There is no government-sanctioned approval process for surgical procedures.) This 80 percent also include applications for drugs doctors prescribe for conditions the drug has not been approved for by the FDA. An example is the drug prednisone—a cortisone-type drug—used for dozens of uses other than for those approved by the FDA.

Whitaker also notes that a majority of cancer and heart disease therapies offer little more than hope and a "big bill."

Now a proponent of less invasive, alternative care therapies, Whitaker says, "The trouble with many excellent, safe and beneficial [natural] therapies is that they cannot be structured into financial powerhouses" referring to those profit-motivated powerhouses of drugs, surgery and other medical care venues.

Whitaker believes this era of health care lies in an "allopathic dark age" where information is suppressed and progress is sidestepped by a government that helps block progress. Individuals in a dark age, he notes, may even consider themselves "enlightened" as they eschew the narrow dogma of the time which is their own truth.[3]

Besides medical doctors like Whitaker and writers like Null, the public, too, is becoming increasingly distrustful of medical care. People can see the priority of the profit motive compared to the quality of care. The high cost of health care and the industry's emphasis on profit bothers an increasingly skeptical public who realizes that their health is likely compromised for medicine's high-priced disease care.

Yet, in the end, health is all there is. Without health there is no life. Without health, there is profit only for those who live long enough to enjoy it. And in the end, many are saying—health practitioners and patients alike—we are fed up and we're not going to take it anymore.

Even though it appears there is no stopping the corporate powers as long as government cooperates in their favor, there is s small voice that is growing more audible with each day. Although it is a voice that was virtually imperceptible at first, it is now gaining credibility, and it promises to alter the future of health care and force an evolution of a new delivery system. This process of change will culminate in a health care delivery system that is vastly different from the system that exists today.

This movement has been called a fringe element because those who practiced it have not been mainstream Americans. Considered unscientific, they have been practicing their forms of therapy quietly in order to avoid the iron fist of the medical dictatorship's far-reaching power.

Most people who sought the care of these practitioners also kept their interests quiet, particularly those who did not want to tell their own medical doctors for fear of being told they were wasting their time and their money and being ignorant besides. Most patients of alternative practitioners wanted to avoid the label of being considered eccentric or foolish.

Yet, in the past few years, particularly since the early 1990s, this trend of silence has begun to change. Preventive (namely nontraditional or alternative) care practitioners are coming out of the closet. Patients are referring their friends, families and co-workers to these practitioners, and open-minded medical doctors are listening and learning, even joining the movement.

Many MD's have been studying and incorporating elements of alternative care into their own practices—taking the best of it and the best of medicine as well. This new breed of medical doctor, joined by the many faceted branches of the holistic health care profession, are creating a radically new kind of care, that, it is predicted, will gradually become mainstream with the transition into the twenty-first century. That care will be prevention oriented, not ruled by the existing focus on disease.

Yet, while these new-thinking medical practitioners deserve credit, the real credit for the evolving system goes to the grassroots effort initiated by people moving away from invasive medical care by choice. The highly profitable medical machine would be content to continue being the only game in town whatever its efficacy, but the public has decided it wants real solutions. People are tired of subsidizing a health care system that is not only expensive and out of reach for many, but one that is not delivering what it has promised—better health. This is the primary reason people are turning their backs on medicine.

In 1993, the medical community learned of this migration of patients toward the alternatives through a study reported in the *New England Journal of Medicine*. The report showed that approximately 33 percent or one-third of the public now seeks the benefits of nonmedical care either in place of or in addition to regular medical care. Or-

thodox medicine's greatest fear is being realized: their position of power is losing ground as the sovereign force it
has enjoyed in the past.[4]

This one-of-three statistic initiated a hesitant, but necessary approval by the medical powers of physicians who
were already pursuing alternative avenues (prevention-
oriented) of health care, or those interested in pursuing
them. The new attitude is that these practitioners should
not be scorned as readily as those who ventured away from
medicine in the past.

Alternative health care books by medical doctors and
nonmedical alternative practitioners have begun filling the
health section shelves at Barnes and Noble and other book-
stores across the country. These books are selling, including titles by Andrew Weil, Deepak Chopra, Robert Arnot as
well as other MDs who have followed MD pioneers into the
alternative field. Books by pioneers like Lendon Smith and
Robert Atkins, whose works had often been crucified by
their colleagues in the past, are gaining readership and
credibility. Nontraditional medical gurus have become
bookselling sensations thanks to a public that has long
waited for health care answers. These people are reaching
out to new avenues for pursuing elusive health. Meanwhile,
books by conventional MDs are simply not selling as they
have in the past.

Despite this progress, medicine's acceptance of alternative care is far from complete. Steps must be taken before orthodox practitioners will hold hands with alternative care to decide on the best treatment for the patient.
However, there is the acceptance of bits and pieces of the
alternative medicine approach under continued public pressure.

As a whole, medicine continues to take swipes at alternative care—homeopathy, chiropractic, clinical nutrition,
mind/body healing—in an attempt to diminish holistic's
reputation as a viable source of quality care and to hold on
to their monopoly as long as possible. Holistic practitioners
are still labelled with euphemisms for "quack," or a simple
smirk and chuckle by those in the medical profession who
hold firm to their own beliefs.

As the struggle for power is played out, there is an ultimate hope that the growing body of medical professionals will keep the best of medicine and accept what is good in alternative care. Particularly the new, younger doctor, who sees medicine's work in shades of gray, not just black and white, is keeping a watchful eye on all protocols—whether approved by the medical establishment or not.

Many say that as the old school of medical professionals retires and leaves the profession, it will be these younger, more open-minded doctors who will usher in the new school of thought, these new doctors who will select from the best of both worlds.

This change in philosophy is exemplified by medical schools and teaching hospitals now including alternative care studies in their curricula. These include Montefiore Medical Center in New York City, Tufts University in Boston, the University of Miami and Columbia University. Columbia University, a traditional medical mainstay until recently, has established the Richard & Hinda Rosenthal Center for Alternative/Complementary Medicine. According to the publication *Health News and Review:*

> By evaluating existing scientific, empirical and anecdotal data on alternative medical practices, Dr. Fredi Kronenberg, the Center's director, hopes to provide a resource for physicians and patients seeking information on such practices as homeopathy, hypnosis, biofeedback, osteopathy, acupuncture, nutritional and vitamin therapy, and mind-body medicine.

One of the Center's first undertakings is a course called "Survey in Alternative and Complementary Medicine," for second-year medical students. Interest in the course was so great that a larger hall was needed for the class. According to Dr. Kronenberg, several of her own colleagues have "come out of the woodwork. Many doctors have this interest [in alternative medicine]; they just never reveal[ed] it to anybody."[5]

There is clearly a blending of traditional and nontraditional care, of medicine and the alternatives in progress. Yet before a better health care system can be established, one additional element must come into play—the element of the individual taking responsibility for his own health.

For too long, medicine has taken both the responsibility and the right away from the patient. By ordering his treatments—his drugs, his surgeries—the doctor has rendered the patient helpless. In this, the medical system had full control of how and when its protocols would be administered. Medicine had complete power. The patient none. That was perhaps the intention in the Hippocratic Oath— to keep knowledge of the patient's condition from him, giving more power to the physician himself. Knowledge is power. Yet today, patients want their share.

Forward-thinking practitioners believe that health is not a therapy; it is not a drug or a surgery. Health is a journey toward a well state of being that changes daily. Anyone is a fool to think that health is anything but tenuous; it requires daily vigilance.

In the book, *Healers on Healing*, noted health pioneers provide their personal views on wellness. Although these noted individuals including Elisabeth Kubler Ross and Norman Cousins deliver their messages from varying perspectives, there is one unified message (paraphrased):

> **Health care needs to be taken away from the doctor, away from the hospital, away from the pharmaceutical industry and every other medical entity, and the responsibility of health given back to the patient, where it belongs. There the individual must make the day-to-day choices that will determine health, whatever those choices are.**[6]

Health is the sum total of every system of the body working in harmony toward wellness. It is not a matter of its individual parts working in isolation. Health cannot be accomplished by a cardiologist performing bypass surgery and caring for the heart as an isolated system, by an oncologist caring for a diseased liver as if it had no connection to the other organs of the body, or by a lifelong spectrum of drugs. Health at its best is achieved by the individual looking after his own body and seeing it as an entire organism, where all systems interact and affect the others. Health is achieved by setting the stage and the environment for wellness, not by trying to retrieve health after it is already lost.

Politicians and those with the "brightest minds" continue to debate the way they believe healthcare should be delivered—who should deliver it and how much it will cost. Lobbyists struggle to have their interests heard and to help their client industries survive. Debates rage over issues such as managed care. Still, the single most vital component of health is greatly neglected and intentionally so by big business interests. That component is the simple concept that health involves a solidarity of the body, of mind and body, of every cell, every system, all which must be orchestrated—cared for—by the individual yet guided by the health care provider. Health care orchestrated by politics or by profit will not allow the individual to survive, will not allow us to own health as our most valued possession.

No matter what healthcare is today or what it becomes tomorrow, the individual must realize that it is his health—her health—that is always in the balance. Only solidarity can maintain health. Only solidarity can keep us whole.

The bottom line, the buck—all powerful to the medical industry—must stop with each person. It must stop here.

1. *Health and Healing*, Andrew Weil, Houghton-Mifflin, 1988.

2. *Your Body Naturally*, Four Walls, Eight Windows, Gary Null, 1992, pg xiv.

3. *Guide to Natural Healing*, Julian Whitaker, MD, Prima Publishing, Rocklin, CA, 1995, pgs xi-xii.

4. *New England Journal of Medicine*, David Eisenberg, MD et al, January 28, 1993.

5. *Health News & Review*, Volume 4, No. 2/1994, pg. 17.

6. *Healers on Healing*, Richard Carlson, Ph.D. and Benjamin Shield, editors, Tarcher/Putnam,1989.

Epilogue

Pharmaceutical sales continue to soar and so, in turn, do industry profits, yet rates of illness continue to soar as well. The success of the former appears to have little effect on the condition of the latter. In spite of the fact that dozens of "better" and almost always more expensive drugs continue to come our way, the health of the general public remains on a decline. The incidence of chronic and debilitating disease increases beyond imagination, robbing millions of people of their quality of life and life itself, and still the drugs keep coming as if even more drugs were the answer. In response, the public gulps down more drugs at an even faster rate.

The Drug Lords win with the complicity of a co-conspirator—the news media—who report in their multiplicity of news programming every "pharmaceutical breakthrough" as if it truly were one. With rarely a trace of dignified investigation or adequate rebuttal on the media's part, reporters regurgitate what the pharmaceutical representatives tell them, spitting out "new findings" almost word for word. After that sales move upward; sometimes they fly upward. The drug industry could ask for no better public relations force. It is only unfortunate that many of those who are listening are desperate for a thread of hope: the woman diagnosed with breast cancer, the young man with

AIDS, the parents of an ill child. That "hope" is the pharmaceutical company's marketing edge, an unfair edge that too often ends in exploitation. The Drug Lords get fatter on the public's misguided trust, a public who has learned to believe the propaganda.

So on it continues: the drug makers continuing to discover new drugs for old problems and creating new markets for existing ones, but the question remains, "At whose expense?" "At what cost?" and especially "For what cure?"

Dateline March 1996

Another alleged breakthrough, this time in the pediatrics field. Prozac, the antidepressant drug that has received so much attention because of its potential to induce pronounced agitation, even violent tendencies, in its users. This same drug Prozac is now being recommended for even very young children to help them with their varied cases of shyness. The news reporter advises patients to "Ask your doctor if Prozac just might be the right solution for your shy son or your shy daughter."

Start them young. Make them lifelong customers of the Drug Lords.

INDEX

No Barriers Publishing
publisher of this book

has created a bi-monthly newsletter to keep watch on the pulse of the healthcare industry. For more information about the newsletter or to request a subscription, write to—

HEALTH INDUSTRY WATCH
1201 S. Westnedge Ave.
Kalamazoo, MI 49008-1349
Tel 800 828-3057
616 344-6038
IM49008@aol.com

ORDER FORM
The Drug Lords...
America's Pharmaceutical Cartel

Order copies of this book by calling toll free 1 800 828-3057. Or use this coupon to order by mail. For quantity discounts, please call for a quote.

Please send *The Drug Lords: America's Pharmaceutical Cartel,* at $12.95 each, plus postage.

Number of copies_____ X $12.95   = $_____
Sales tax (in Michigan) 6%   = $_____
Postage & handling   = $_____
  ($2 for the first copy, $0.50
  for each additional book)
Total amount enclosed   = $_____
Send to:

_____(___)_____
Name   Telephone

_____
Address

_____
City   State   Zip Code

Send check, money order or VISA/MC/Discover Card information to:

      No Barriers Publishing
      1201 S. Westnedge Ave.
      Kalamazoo, MI 49008-1349

Credit card #_____Expiration date_____

Signature of cardholder_____

Note: Prices and numbers subject to change without notice. Valid in the U.S. only. For international orders, please call 616 344-6038 for rates. All orders subject to availability.